TOUCHPOINTS™

for Students

Books in the
TOUCHPOINTS™
Series

CP0270

TYNDALE HOUSE PUBLISHERS, INC.
CAROL STREAM, ILLINOIS

TouchPoints™
FOR STUDENTS
Second Edition

Visit Tyndale's exciting Web site at www.tyndale.com.

TYNDALE, *New Living Translation*, *NLT*, the New Living Translation logo, and Tyndale's quill logo are registered trademarks of Tyndale House Publishers, Inc.

TouchPoints is a trademark of Tyndale House Publishers, Inc.

TouchPoints for Students

Questions, notes, and Scripture selection primarily by Jonathan Gray

Contributing writers: V. Gilbert Beers, Rebecca Beers, Brian R. Coffey, Jonathan Farrar, Jonathan Gray, Sean A. Harrison, Sandy Hull, Amy E. Mason, Rhonda K. O'Brien, Douglas J. Rumford, Linda Taylor

Previously published under ISBN-13: 978-0-8423-3308-5

Designed by Jennifer Ghionzoli

ISBN 978-1-4143-2021-2

Printed in the United States of America

15 14 13 12
 8   7   6   5   4

INTRODUCTION ◄●

PSALM 119:105 | *Your word is a lamp to guide my feet and a light for my path.*

PSALM 119:111, 162 | *Your laws are my treasure; they are my heart's delight. . . . I rejoice in your word like one who discovers a great treasure.*

PSALM 119:91, 160 | *Your regulations remain true to this day, for everything serves your plans. . . . The very essence of your words is truth; all your just regulations will stand forever.*

What a treasure we have in the living Word of God! The Holy Bible is relevant to today's issues and gives solid guidance for daily living. In this book you will find over one hundred topics that apply to your everyday life as well as what the Bible says about each one. The topics are presented alphabetically, along with several questions, Scriptures, and comments addressing each one. In the table of contents in the front of this book you will find a complete listing of all of them for quick reference. While we could not cover all topics, questions, and Scriptures related to students, the subject of this book, our prayer is that you will continue to deliberately search God's Word to grow closer to him and discover how his way of living is the best path to joy and satisfaction. Whether you read through this book page by page or you use it as a reference guide for topics of particular interest to you, may you find answers in God's Word as he longs to be your daily Guide.

Enjoy your treasure hunt.

The editors

2 TIMOTHY 3:16 | *All Scripture is inspired by God and is useful to teach us what is true and to make us realize what is wrong in our lives. It corrects us when we are wrong and teaches us to do what is right.*

CONTENTS

ABSENCE

Why do I sometimes feel that God is absent?

PSALM 10:1 | *O LORD, why do you stand so far away? Why do you hide when I am in trouble?*

PSALM 139:2, 7 | *You know when I sit down or stand up. You know my thoughts even when I'm far away. . . . I can never escape from your Spirit! I can never get away from your presence!*

The greater your troubles, the farther away God sometimes seems. In your darkest hour, you may feel that God has left you. In times like this, when it seems as if God is absent, don't trust your feelings; trust God's promise that he will never leave you. Rely on what the Bible tells you is true, not on what your feelings are telling you.

ISAIAH 59:1-2 | *Listen! The LORD's arm is not too weak to save you, nor is his ear too deaf to hear you call. It's your sins that have cut you off from God.*

When God seems far away, it may be because you have moved away from him, not because he has moved away from you. Sometimes there might be a sin you are not willing to let go of that causes you to feel cut off from God and miss the joy of friendship with him. Is there some sin that is keeping you from moving toward God? Tear down the wall of sin by confessing it to God, and you will find him on the other side.

Promise from God   MATTHEW 28:20 | *[Jesus said,] "Be sure of this: I am with you always, even to the end of the age."*

ABSOLUTES

There seems to be so many gray areas when it comes to right and wrong. How can I tell what is really right?

EXODUS 20:1 | *God gave the people all these instructions.*

JOHN 14:15 | *[Jesus said,] "If you love me, obey my commandments."*

God has given you his Word, the Bible, which clearly tells you the things that are absolutely right and absolutely wrong.

ROMANS 8:5 | *Those who are dominated by the sinful nature think about sinful things, but those who are controlled by the Holy Spirit think about things that please the Spirit.*

GALATIANS 5:16 | *Let the Holy Spirit guide your lives. Then you won't be doing what your sinful nature craves.*

God has given you the Holy Spirit, who will help you live obediently and teach you absolute truth, even when your old sinful nature is trying to take over and distort the truth.

Some friends make fun of me for doing right. How do I deal with that?

ROMANS 2:10 | *There will be glory and honor and peace from God for all who do good.*

1 PETER 3:14 | *If you suffer for doing what is right, God will reward you for it.*

Have you ever wondered why you feel good after doing something you know is right? That peace is God's reward to you for doing what is right.

Why do I need absolutes? Can't I just do my own thing?

JUDGES 21:25 | *In those days Israel had no king; all the people did whatever seemed right in their own eyes.*

PROVERBS 21:2 | *People may be right in their own eyes, but the LORD examines their heart.*

JAMES 4:11 | *Your job is to obey the law, not to judge whether it applies to you.*

From the beginning of time, people who did what was right in their own eyes reaped catastrophic consequences for themselves and others. The Bible teaches that you are born with the desire to sin, so doing your own thing will always lead you away from God. Your job is not to pass judgment on God's ways by devising your own, but to follow God and all he says. If you buy something that needs assembling, and you purposely go against the instruction manual, what you assemble will not work properly. It's the same with life. Follow God's instruction manual, the Bible.

Promise from God   2 TIMOTHY 3:16 | *All Scripture is inspired by God and is useful to teach us what is true and to make us realize what is wrong in our lives. It corrects us when we are wrong and teaches us to do what is right.*

ACCEPTANCE

What makes me acceptable to God?

ROMANS 3:27 | *Can we boast, then, that we have done anything to be accepted by God? No, because our acquittal is not based on obeying the law. It is based on faith.*

No one can earn God's acceptance. Nothing you do could ever compensate for your sin. The only way to be accepted by God is to believe that his Son, Jesus, died for your sins so that you could be free to enjoy eternal life with him. When you accept his forgiveness and let him be Lord of your life, he completely accepts you into his presence. It's that simple.

What if a person has committed a terrible sin? Should I still accept him or her?

ROMANS 8:39 | *Nothing . . . will ever be able to separate us from the love of God that is revealed in Christ Jesus our Lord.*

Nothing can separate a person from God's love. In the same way, you should always love others, no matter how great their sin. This does not mean that you accept or condone their sinful actions or ignore the appropriate discipline but that you view and accept them as unique and special creations of God. It is only through love that you bring sinful people back into fellowship with God and others.

How do I learn to accept those who are different from me?

MATTHEW 9:11-12 | *The Pharisees . . . asked [Jesus'] disciples, "Why does your teacher eat with such scum?" When Jesus heard this, he said, "Healthy people don't need a doctor— sick people do."*

Every person is a unique creation of God and is loved by God. If God loves everyone, shouldn't you?

Promise from God ROMANS 15:7 | *Accept each other just as Christ has accepted you so that God will be given glory.*

ACCOMPLISHMENTS

What is the right perspective on my accomplishments?

ECCLESIASTES 12:13 | *Here now is my final conclusion: Fear God and obey his commands, for this is everyone's duty.*

Obeying God is life's greatest accomplishment.

ROMANS 1:17 | *This Good News tells us how God makes us right in his sight. This is accomplished from start to finish by faith. As the Scriptures say, "It is through faith that a righteous person has life."*

Salvation, the greatest of accomplishments, is not accomplished through your own work but through the work of God in your heart. It is simply by faith: believing that Jesus Christ died for your sins so that you can live forever with him.

How can I achieve my God-given potential?

JOHN 5:19 | *Jesus explained, "I tell you the truth, the Son can do nothing by himself. He does only what he sees the Father doing. Whatever the Father does, the Son also does."*

JOHN 15:5 | *[Jesus said,] "I am the vine; you are the branches. Those who remain in me, and I in them, will produce much fruit. For apart from me you can do nothing."*

By staying in a healthy relationship with God. The product of a growing relationship with God is a deepened faith in who he is and what he can do. Achieving your God-given potential means accepting what God has given you to do and using his power to accomplish it.

Is it wrong to be proud of my accomplishments?

1 CORINTHIANS 4:7 | *What gives you the right to make such a judgment? What do you have that God hasn't given you? And if everything you have is from God, why boast as though it were not a gift?*

Accomplishment brings a healthy sense of satisfaction, which then should lead you to thank God for what he has done through you.

How do I make the most of my accomplishments?

ECCLESIASTES 4:9 | *Two people are better off than one, for they can help each other succeed.*

Accomplishments are multiplied through a team. You can't play football or soccer without teamwork. How encouraging to note that two people can do more than twice as much as one, as long as they are pulling in the same direction!

What is a good model for accomplishing things?

ISAIAH 25:1 | *O Lord, I will honor and praise your name, for you are my God. You do such wonderful things! You planned them long ago, and now you have accomplished them.*

Accomplishments follow good planning. God planned before he accomplished—a good model for you to follow.

Promise from God PSALM 60:12 | *With God's help we will do mighty things.*

ACCOUNTABILITY

Why is accountability so important?

ECCLESIASTES 4:9-10, 12 | *Two people are better off than one, for they can help each other succeed. If one person falls, the other can reach out and help. But someone who falls alone is in real trouble. . . . A person standing alone can be attacked and defeated, but two can stand back-to-back and conquer. Three are even better, for a triple-braided cord is not easily broken.*

A person standing alone against the world is vulnerable. You need mutual support and companionship. Enlisting a Christian friend as an accountability partner will more than double your spiritual strength. Include the Lord in that relationship and you become "triple-braided."

How do I become more accountable?

JEREMIAH 23:24 | *"Can anyone hide from me in a secret place? Am I not everywhere in all the heavens and earth?" says the LORD.*

If you're going to take accountability seriously, you have to begin with God. You will better understand what you are doing and why you are doing it when you understand for whom you are doing it. God knows all the secrets of your heart anyway, so why try to hide anything from him? Be honest with him; tell him the struggles you have in following him.

PSALM 119:9, 66 | *How can a young person stay pure? By obeying your word. . . . I believe in your commands; now teach me good judgment and knowledge.*

To become more accountable, follow God's commands as outlined in his Word, the Bible.

PSALM 1:1 | *Oh, the joys of those who do not follow the advice of the wicked, or stand around with sinners, or join in with mockers.*

PROVERBS 27:6 | *Wounds from a sincere friend are better than many kisses from an enemy.*

Purposefully choose wise friends who will hold you accountable. Their honesty may hurt at times but can save you from greater pain down the road.

Does God really hold me accountable for all my actions?

ECCLESIASTES 11:9 | *Young people, it's wonderful to be young! Enjoy every minute of it. Do everything you want to do; take it all in. But remember that you must give an account to God for everything you do.*

Enjoy life, but stay within God's guidelines. Live today as though you will be with God in eternity tomorrow. Yes, God will hold you accountable for everything you do, and who wants to try to explain ungodliness to a holy God on the Day of Judgment?

JEREMIAH 12:2-3 | *Your name is on their lips, but you are far from their hearts. But as for me, LORD, you know my heart. You see me and test my thoughts.*

Others may be able to judge your actions, but only God knows your motives, thoughts, and feelings.

How can I effectively hold someone else accountable?

EXODUS 18:21-22 | *Select from all the people some capable, honest men who fear God and hate bribes. . . . They will help you carry the load, making the task easier for you.*

Before you can help others be accountable, you must not only know God's commands but be committed to obeying them yourself. You must also be able to use good judgment. If you are going to hold others accountable, you must work to be wise, honest, godly, trustworthy, and kind.

How can I choose the right people to hold me accountable?

1 KINGS 12:8, 10-11 | *Rehoboam rejected the advice of the older men and instead asked the opinion of the young men who had grown up with him. . . . The young men replied, "This is what you should tell those complainers . . . 'Yes, my father laid heavy*

burdens on you, but I'm going to make them even heavier! My father beat you with whips, but I will beat you with scorpions!'"

Your closest friends may not always be the best advisers, especially if their counsel is not consistent with God's Word.

1 CORINTHIANS 12:8 | *To one person the Spirit gives the ability to give wise advice; to another the same Spirit gives a message of special knowledge.*

Choose people who are especially wise and godly, who will not hesitate to help you see when you need to realign yourself with God.

What happens when there is no accountability?

JUDGES 17:6 | *In those days Israel had no king; all the people did whatever seemed right in their own eyes.*

Left unaccountable, people will always lean toward sin, which eventually hurts them and others and pulls them away from God. This could happen to you, as well.

Promise from God PSALM 37:30 | *The godly offer good counsel; they teach right from wrong.*

ADDICTION

Am I addicted?

ROMANS 6:12 | *Do not let sin control the way you live; do not give in to sinful desires.*

JOHN 8:34 | *Jesus replied, "I tell you the truth, everyone who sins is a slave of sin."*

2 PETER 2:19 | *You are a slave to whatever controls you.*

You become addicted when you let something control you. Sin, your greatest addiction, is often alluring and attractive, offering short-term pleasure. It is easy to justify giving in "just this once," because you think you have things under control. But soon you realize that what you are giving in to has become a habit you can't break. It is now controlling you. Sin's control often comes from the loss of self-control.

How can God break the power of addiction in my life?

GALATIANS 5:22-23 | *The Holy Spirit produces this kind of fruit in our lives: love, joy, peace, patience, kindness, goodness, faithfulness, gentleness, and self-control.*

God breaks the power of addiction when you give him control of your life. He will come into your life and change your heart and your desires. Surrender to the Holy Spirit, and God will replace addictive drives with life-affirming desires.

ROMANS 6:16 | *Don't you realize that you become the slave of whatever you choose to obey? You can be a slave to sin, which leads to death, or you can choose to obey God, which leads to righteous living.*

Submission is a choice to obey something or someone. Every day you stand at a crossroads, choosing sinful ways or God's way. The choice is yours. Admit your need to God in prayer, release all your anxieties to him, and rely fully on the promise of God's help.

EPHESIANS 5:18 | *Don't be drunk with wine, because that will ruin your life. Instead, be filled with the Holy Spirit.*

It is imperative to admit your addiction and acknowledge its destructiveness. While it is healthy and important to seek the help of others, with God's help you have the ultimate power to overcome addiction.

PROVERBS 13:14 | *The instruction of the wise is like a life-giving fountain; those who accept it avoid the snares of death.*

It is almost impossible to overcome addiction by yourself. You need the consistent support of other people who love you, tell you the truth, and hold you accountable. Participating in an addiction-recovery support group is often valuable, perhaps even essential, in order to overcome an addiction. God often works through other people to help you.

ROMANS 12:2 | *Don't copy the behavior and customs of this world, but let God transform you into a new person by changing the way you think. Then you will learn to know God's will for you, which is good and pleasing and perfect.*

Freedom from addiction comes as you change your focus and the way you think. You do this by trusting Christ to transform you and give you the power to resist temptation.

Promise from God ROMANS 6:16 | *Don't you realize that you become the slave of whatever you choose to obey? You can be a slave to sin, which leads to death, or you can choose to obey God, which leads to righteous living.*

ADVICE

Do I need advice from others? Why can't I just rely on my own wisdom?

PROVERBS 12:15 | *Fools think their own way is right, but the wise listen to others.*

Wisdom is recognizing your own inadequacies. Foolishness is thinking you have none. It is better to recognize your limitations and seek good counsel at the beginning of a problem than to discover that your limitations have made the situation worse. Avoid getting into a position where you say to yourself, *If only I had asked someone sooner.*

Where do I look for good advice?

PSALM 37:30 | *The godly offer good counsel; they teach right from wrong.*

COLOSSIANS 3:16 | *Let the message about Christ, in all its richness, fill your lives. Teach and counsel each other with all the wisdom he gives.*

First, look for advice from God through prayer and by reading his Word. Next, seek advice from godly people who have the gift of wisdom. These are people who have proven themselves to be faithful, godly, honest, and trustworthy.

How do I evaluate the advice of others?

2 JOHN 1:9 | *Anyone who wanders away from this teaching has no relationship with God. But anyone who remains in the teaching of Christ has a relationship with both the Father and the Son.*

MATTHEW 7:16, 20 | *You can identify them by their fruit, that is, by the way they act. . . . Yes, just as you can identify a tree by its fruit, so you can identify people by their actions.*

One way to test advice is to evaluate the advisers. Do their actions match their words? Does their advice square with the truth of God's Word? If it contradicts the Bible, it's bad advice.

How do I give good advice to others?

PHILIPPIANS 4:8 | *Fix your thoughts on what is true, and honorable, and right, and pure, and lovely, and admirable. Think about things that are excellent and worthy of praise.*

In giving advice, make sure your motives are right—to offer the best possible advice for the situation, not to offer advice that might improve your own situation. Point to the Bible, and don't use advice as an excuse to lecture. Pray about what you need to say, and have the other person's best interests in mind.

How valuable is wise advice?

PROVERBS 25:11 | *Timely advice is lovely, like golden apples in a silver basket.*

Timely advice is not merely helpful; it is beautiful and essential because it comes just when you need it. Having a godly counselor to coach you at your time of need is a blessing because it helps you avoid pain and heartache.

Promise from God PSALM 32:8 | *The LORD says, "I will guide you along the best pathway for your life. I will advise you and watch over you."*

AIDS

Why is there AIDS?

GENESIS 3:19 | *By the sweat of your brow will you have food to eat until you return to the ground from which you were made. For you were made from dust, and to dust you will return.*

When Adam and Eve disobeyed God, sin entered the world and all of life changed. As a result, there are sickness, pain, and death. AIDS, like any disease, is one of the results of living in a fallen world.

What should my response and responsibility be to people with AIDS?

MATTHEW 22:39 | *Love your neighbor as yourself.*

MARK 6:34 | *Jesus saw the huge crowd as he stepped from the boat, and he had compassion on them.*

ROMANS 12:9 | *Don't just pretend to love others. Really love them. Hate what is wrong. Hold tightly to what is good.*

2 CORINTHIANS 1:4 | *He comforts us in all our troubles so that we can comfort others. When they are troubled, we will be able to give them the same comfort God has given us.*

2 CORINTHIANS 2:6-7 | *Most of you opposed [the man who caused all the trouble], and that was punishment enough. Now, however, it is time to forgive and comfort him. Otherwise he may be overcome by discouragement.*

Regardless of how people with AIDS acquired it, Scripture commands you to treat them with the same love that Christ would show them. This does not mean you condone immoral lifestyle choices, but the love of Christ must be shown equally to all people. Only then can God's message of grace and forgiveness and healing break through. God calls you to love, serve, and have compassion for all people.

Promise from God   2 CORINTHIANS 1:4 | *He comforts us in all our troubles so that we can comfort others.*

ANGER

Why do I get angry?

GENESIS 4:4-5 | *The LORD accepted Abel and his gift, but he did not accept Cain and his gift. This made Cain very angry, and he looked dejected.*

NUMBERS 22:29 | *"You have made me look like a fool!" Balaam shouted.*

2 CHRONICLES 26:18-19 | *[The priests] confronted King Uzziah and said, "It is not for you, Uzziah, to burn incense to the LORD. That is the work of the priests alone, the descendants of Aaron who are set apart for this work. Get out of the sanctuary, for you have sinned. The LORD God will not honor you for this!" Uzziah, who was holding an incense burner, became furious.*

ESTHER 3:5 | *When Haman saw that Mordecai would not bow down or show him respect, he was filled with rage.*

Anger is often a reaction to hurt pride. When you are confronted, rejected, ignored, or don't get your own way, anger is a defense mechanism used to protect your ego. It is common to feel angry when you have been confronted about your own sinful actions, because you don't want others to think you have done something wrong.

1 SAMUEL 18:8 | *Saul [became] very angry. "What's this?" he said. "They credit David with ten thousands and me with only thousands. Next they'll be making him their king!"*

Anger is often a reaction of jealousy to what others have or to what others have accomplished.

When is anger appropriate?

JOHN 2:15-16 | *Jesus . . . drove out the sheep and cattle, scattered the money changers' coins over the floor, and turned over their tables. Then, going over to the people who sold doves, he told them, "Get these things out of here. Stop turning my Father's house into a marketplace!"*

Jesus' righteous anger came from his devotion to God and from his compassion for others. It led to good deeds, not bad. Anger at sin is not only appropriate but necessary.

When I am angry, what should I avoid?

JAMES 3:5 | *The tongue is a small thing that makes grand speeches. But a tiny spark can set a great forest on fire.*

Avoid "speaking your mind" when you are angry. You are bound to say something you will regret.

1 SAMUEL 19:9-10 | *As David played his harp, Saul hurled his spear at David.*

Avoid acting on impulse in the heat of anger. You are bound to do something you will regret.

Promise from God PSALM 103:8-9 | *The LORD is compassionate and merciful, slow to get angry and filled with unfailing love. He will not constantly accuse us, nor remain angry forever.*

APATHY

What causes apathy?

PROVERBS 29:7 | *The godly care about the rights of the poor; the wicked don't care at all.*

EPHESIANS 4:18-19 | *Their minds are full of darkness; they wander far from the life God gives because they have closed their minds and hardened their hearts against him. They have no sense of shame. They live for lustful pleasure and eagerly practice every kind of impurity.*

Sinful living causes apathy. Sin turns the spotlight on self and selfishness, so concern for others fades away.

DEUTERONOMY 6:11-12 | *The houses will be richly stocked with goods you did not produce. You will draw water from cisterns you did not dig, and you will eat from vineyards and olive trees you did not plant. When you have eaten your fill in this land, be careful not to forget the LORD, who rescued you from slavery in the land of Egypt.*

Success can lead to apathy. Preoccupation with material things eventually leads to apathy because earthly things have no lasting value.

What happens if apathy is allowed to grow in my life?

JEREMIAH 12:4 | *How long must this land mourn? Even the grass in the fields has withered. The wild animals and birds have disappeared because of the evil in the land.*

When you are apathetic, life ultimately becomes empty and withered because you wonder if anything you've done really matters or will really last. When you invite God into your life, he begins to clean out the weeds of apathy so the landscape of your soul can thrive and flourish.

Promise from God 2 TIMOTHY 1:7 | *God has not given us a spirit of fear and timidity, but of power, love, and self-discipline.*

APPEARANCE

How important to God is my outward appearance?

1 SAMUEL 16:7 | *People judge by outward appearance, but the LORD looks at the heart.*

PROVERBS 31:30 | *Charm is deceptive, and beauty does not last; but a woman who fears the LORD will be greatly praised.*

God focuses on your heart and your relationship with him; not on your outward appearance. Though it is important to take care of your body, it is more important to God that you focus on becoming beautiful on the inside. Walking with God causes you to reflect his beauty from within.

1 CORINTHIANS 6:19 | *Don't you realize that your body is the temple of the Holy Spirit, who lives in you and was given to you by God?*

You should not be obsessed with your physical appearance, but neither should you ignore it. Your body is the house in which the Holy Spirit dwells, so you should keep up the place in which he lives. The more you keep up your body, the more energy you have to serve him.

Can I trust people based on their appearance?

ISAIAH 53:3 | *He was despised and rejected—a man of sorrows, acquainted with deepest grief. We turned our backs on him and looked the other way. He was despised, and we did not care.*

MATTHEW 23:28 | *Outwardly you look like righteous people, but inwardly your hearts are filled with hypocrisy and lawlessness.*

What you see is not always what you get. Appearances can be misleading. Jesus came to earth as a plain-looking man and was not recognized as God's Son despite the perfect condition of his heart. Be careful not to judge people based on how they look.

Promise from God 1 SAMUEL 16:7 | *People judge by outward appearance, but the LORD looks at the heart.*

APPROVAL

Do I have to earn God's approval?

ROMANS 8:39 | *No power in the sky above or in the earth below—indeed, nothing in all creation will ever be able to separate us from the love of God that is revealed in Christ Jesus our Lord.*

GALATIANS 2:19 | *[Paul said,] "When I tried to keep the law, it condemned me. So I died to the law—I stopped trying to meet all its requirements—so that I might live for God."*

You cannot earn God's approval, because he already approves of you! His approval is not based on your performance but on the fact that you are his creation. Your performance is an expression of gratitude to God, not the basis for his approval.

If God's approval is not earned, how can I receive it?

JOHN 3:16 | *God loved the world so much that he gave his one and only Son, so that everyone who believes in him will not perish but have eternal life.*

HEBREWS 11:5 | *It was by faith that Enoch was taken up to heaven without dying—"he disappeared, because God took him." For before he was taken up, he was known as a person who pleased God.*

You receive God's approval by believing that Jesus Christ is God's only Son and that Jesus died on the cross for your sins so you can have eternal life in heaven with him. There is nothing else you need to do!

Promise from God ROMANS 15:7 | *Accept each other just as Christ has accepted you so that God will be given glory.*

ASTROLOGY

Is astrology wrong?

EXODUS 20:3 | *[The Lord said,] "You must not have any other god but me."*

2 KINGS 21:6 | *Manasseh . . . practiced sorcery and divination, and he consulted with mediums and psychics. He did much that was evil in the LORD's sight, arousing his anger.*

Astrology is wrong because it worships the heavens instead of the God who created the heavens. And worshiping anything or anyone other than God is idolatry.

Can astrology give me direction?

GENESIS 1:16-17 | *God made two great lights—the larger one to govern the day, and the smaller one to govern the night. He also made the stars. God set these lights in the sky to light the earth.*

Don't look for advice from the stars but rather from God, the Creator of the stars. Only he can give you direction for your life because he created you, too. You should never worship the Creation over the Creator. God controls all celestial events; only he can point you in the right direction.

Promise from God ISAIAH 45:18 | *The LORD is God, and he created the heavens and earth and put everything in place. He made the world to be lived in, not to be a place of empty chaos. "I am the LORD," he says, "and there is no other."*

BACKSLIDING

What do I do when I've fallen away from God?

AMOS 5:4 | *This is what the LORD says to the family of Israel: "Come back to me and live!"*

ROMANS 3:23-24 | *Everyone has sinned; we all fall short of God's glorious standard. Yet God, with undeserved kindness, declares that we are righteous.*

1 JOHN 1:9 | *If we confess our sins to him, he is faithful and just to forgive us our sins and to cleanse us from all wickedness.*

It will happen to you, as it does to almost everyone from time to time. You'll suddenly realize you are farther from God than you should be. It worries you, maybe scares you. Don't ignore that internal warning. Find out what happened—was it simple neglect, or more likely, was it a sinful habit that you didn't want to give up? Only when you recognize what you've done can you confess it to God, and only by confessing can you be forgiven and begin the process of restoring your relationship with him. Confession is the act of acknowledging that your sin has separated you from God. The request for forgiveness is your verbal expression that you want to move back toward him. The extension of forgiveness is God's act of bringing you back to him.

How can I avoid backsliding?

MATTHEW 26:41 | *Keep watch and pray, so that you will not give in to temptation. For the spirit is willing, but the body is weak!*

1 CORINTHIANS 10:13 | *The temptations in your life are no different from what others experience. And God is faithful. He will not allow the temptation to be more than you can stand. When you are tempted, he will show you a way out so that you can endure.*

1 PETER 1:14 | *You must live as God's obedient children. Don't slip back into your old ways of living to satisfy your own desires.*

To avoid backsliding, read the Bible regularly and pray often throughout the day. When temptation comes, walk away from it as quickly as possible. Don't look longingly at what is tempting you.

What is the effect on others when I backslide?

MATTHEW 18:7 | *What sorrow awaits the world, because it tempts people to sin. Temptations are inevitable, but what sorrow awaits the person who does the tempting.*

When you sin, it almost always affects someone besides yourself. And you might tempt someone who is watching you to sin as well. Then your sin has doubled in effect. Like a pebble tossed into a quiet pool, one small sin may reach out in ever-widening circles of influence that can never be reversed.

Promise from God PSALM 32:5 | *Finally, I confessed all my sins to you. . . . And you forgave me!*

BEHAVIOR

Why is godly behavior important?

MATTHEW 5:16 | *Let your good deeds shine out for all to see, so that everyone will praise your heavenly Father.*

LUKE 11:28 | *Jesus [said], "Blessed are all who hear the word of God and put it into practice."*

ROMANS 13:13 | *Don't participate in the darkness of wild parties and drunkenness, or in sexual promiscuity and immoral living, or in quarreling and jealousy.*

Faith in Jesus alone is enough for salvation, but the evidence that your faith is genuine is seen through your behavior. If your sinful behavior doesn't change after you come to faith, then was your confession of faith really genuine when you asked God to forgive your sins, enter your life, and transform who you are? When people see godly behavior in you, they will want to know what makes you different. You then have a wonderful opportunity to tell them, and God promises blessings when you do.

What does God expect in my behavior?

1 TIMOTHY 4:12 | *Don't let anyone think less of you because you are young. Be an example to all believers in what you say, in the way you live, in your love, your faith, and your purity.*

God wants you to be an example to others by the way you live. Therefore, as much as possible, try to live like Jesus.

ROMANS 12:2 | *Don't copy the behavior and customs of this world, but let God transform you into a new person by changing the way you think.*

If you allow God's Spirit to literally transform your behavior, you should be able to live by high standards that seem almost impossible in the eyes of those who aren't yet transformed.

Promise from God LUKE 11:28 | *Blessed are all who hear the word of God and put it into practice.*

BIBLE

How can a book written so long ago be relevant for me today?

ISAIAH 40:8 | *The grass withers and the flowers fade, but the word of our God stands forever.*

2 TIMOTHY 3:16-17 | *All Scripture is inspired by God and is useful to teach us what is true and to make us realize what is wrong in our lives. It corrects us when we are wrong and teaches us to do what is right. God uses it to prepare and equip his people to do every good work.*

HEBREWS 4:12 | *The word of God is alive and powerful. It is sharper than the sharpest two-edged sword, cutting between soul and spirit, between joint and marrow. It exposes our innermost thoughts and desires.*

Because the Bible is the Word of God, it is the only document that is "living"; in other words, it is relevant for all people in all places in any time period. It is as contemporary as the heart of God and as relevant as your most urgent need.

Why is it important to memorize verses from the Bible?

DEUTERONOMY 30:14 | *The message is very close at hand; it is on your lips and in your heart so that you can obey it.*

PSALM 37:31 | *[The godly] have made God's law their own, so they will never slip from his path.*

PSALM 119:11 | *I have hidden your word in my heart, that I might not sin against you.*

What you fill your heart and mind with is what you become. Memorizing Scripture allows you to meditate on God's life-changing words at any time.

How can the Bible give me guidance?

DEUTERONOMY 32:47 | *These instructions are not empty words—they are your life!*

PSALM 119:105 | *Your word is a lamp to guide my feet and a light for my path.*

JAMES 1:5 | *If you need wisdom, ask our generous God, and he will give it to you. He will not rebuke you for asking.*

The Word of God is from the mind and heart of God, who loves you unconditionally and is all-wise, all-powerful, and ever-present.

How can the Bible give me comfort?

PSALM 119:49-50, 52, 54 | *Remember your promise to me; it is my only hope. Your promise revives me; it comforts me in all my troubles. . . . I meditate on your age-old regulations; O LORD, they comfort me. . . . Your decrees have been the theme of my songs wherever I have lived.*

ROMANS 15:4 | *The Scriptures give us hope and encouragement as we wait patiently for God's promises to be fulfilled.*

The Bible is filled with God's promises, which give you comfort and encouragement in this life and the confident assurance that you will one day live forever in peace and security with him.

How often should I read the Bible?

JOSHUA 1:8 | *Study this Book of Instruction continually. Meditate on it day and night so you will be sure to obey everything written in it. Only then will you prosper and succeed in all you do.*

The Bible is for regular reading and meditation in order to learn all you can about God and to communicate with him. If at all possible, this should be done daily. When God says "continually" study his Word, he doesn't mean reading the Bible just when you get around to it.

Promise from God PSALM 119:89 | *Your eternal word, O LORD, stands firm in heaven.*

BITTERNESS

How do I become bitter?

GENESIS 27:41 | *From that time on, Esau hated Jacob because their father had given Jacob the blessing. And Esau began to scheme.*

ESTHER 5:9 | *Haman was a happy man as he left the banquet! But when he saw Mordecai sitting at the palace gate, not standing up or trembling nervously before him, Haman became furious.*

Bitterness grows as you allow anger and then hatred to control you.

2 SAMUEL 2:26 | *Abner shouted down to Joab, "Must we always be killing each other? Don't you realize that bitterness is the only result? When will you call off your men from chasing their Israelite brothers?"*

Bitterness grows the more you retaliate for wrongs done against you.

COLOSSIANS 3:13 | *Make allowance for each other's faults, and forgive anyone who offends you. Remember, the Lord forgave you, so you must forgive others.*

Bitterness comes when others hurt you and you refuse to forgive. Never stop forgiving and forgetting. Remember that God has forgiven you despite your tendency to continually sin.

HEBREWS 12:15 | *Look after each other so that none of you fails to receive the grace of God. Watch out that no poisonous root of bitterness grows up to trouble you, corrupting many.*

Bitterness comes when you forget God's grace, which is showered on you each day.

How do I deal with my bitterness toward others?

MARK 11:25 | *When you are praying, first forgive anyone you are holding a grudge against, so that your Father in heaven will forgive your sins, too.*

EPHESIANS 4:31-32 | *Get rid of all bitterness. . . . Instead, be kind to each other, tenderhearted, forgiving one another, just as God through Christ has forgiven you.*

Forgiveness is the antidote to bitterness. It lifts burdens, cancels debts, and frees you from the chains of unresolved anger.

PHILIPPIANS 1:12-14 | *[Paul said,] "I want you to know, my dear brothers and sisters, that everything that has happened to me here has helped to spread the Good News. . . . Because of my imprisonment, most of the believers here have gained confidence and boldly speak God's message without fear."*

Paul was traveling the world spreading the good news about Jesus. Then he was thrown into prison for sharing his faith! That could have made him bitter. Instead, he was joyful because he saw it as an opportunity. He knew that God takes even the worst situations and, if we allow him to, brings good out of them. Paul couldn't wait to see the good that God would bring out of his prison time. While in prison, Paul wrote many of the New Testament letters, which have brought countless millions to faith in Jesus.

Promise from God   ISAIAH 26:3 | *You will keep in perfect peace all who trust in you, all whose thoughts are fixed on you!*

BLAME

What should I do when I feel like blaming someone else?

MALACHI 2:14 | *You cry out, "Why doesn't the LORD accept my worship?" I'll tell you why! Because the LORD witnessed the vows you and your wife made when you were young. But you have been unfaithful to her, though she remained your faithful partner, the wife of your marriage vows.*

Malachi was explaining to the people of Israel that God hadn't abandoned them; rather, they had abandoned God by their actions (in this case, divorcing their wives and leaving them destitute). Before you blame someone else, especially God, consider how you might be the cause of your problem.

2 SAMUEL 12:13 | *David confessed to Nathan, "I have sinned against the LORD."*

MICAH 6:8 | *O people, the LORD has told you what is good, and this is what he requires of you: to do what is right, to love mercy, and to walk humbly with your God.*

GALATIANS 6:5 | *We are each responsible for our own conduct.*

Be honest in assessing your motives and actions instead of automatically blaming someone else. Sometimes you are not to blame for your problems. You live in a fallen world where pain and suffering come to everyone. When you do something wrong, it's wrong when you don't accept responsibility for your actions. But it's just as wrong to blame yourself for trouble that isn't your fault. When you blame yourself for something you didn't do, you carry a load of guilt that isn't yours to carry.

What can I do to live a blameless life?

1 CORINTHIANS 1:8 | *He will keep you strong to the end so that you will be free from all blame on the day when our Lord Jesus Christ returns.*

COLOSSIANS 1:22 | *[God] has reconciled you to himself through the death of Christ in his physical body. As a result, he has brought you into his own presence, and you are holy and blameless as you stand before him without a single fault.*

1 THESSALONIANS 3:13 | *May he, as a result, make your hearts strong, blameless, and holy as you stand before God our Father when our Lord Jesus comes again with all his holy people.*

There is no way that you, by your own efforts, can ever live a blameless life. It is only through the death of Jesus Christ on the cross that you become blameless in his eyes. When you accept Jesus as Lord of your life and confess your sins to him, his forgiveness cleanses you on the inside. He took on the blame that you deserve. This doesn't mean that you no longer sin but that God looks at you as though you have not sinned.

Promise from God 1 THESSALONIANS 3:13 | *May he . . . make your hearts strong, blameless, and holy as you stand before God our Father when our Lord Jesus comes again with all his holy people.*

BODY

Isn't my body my own, to do with as I choose? Don't I have the final say?

1 CORINTHIANS 6:19-20 | *Don't you realize that your body is the temple of the Holy Spirit, who lives in you and was given to you by God? You do not belong to yourself, for God bought you with a high price. So you must honor God with your body.*

You don't own your body—God does. He paid for you at a premium price with the death of his own Son. Honor his sacrifice with one of your own—respect the awesomeness of your body by keeping it pure.

1 CORINTHIANS 3:16-17 | *Don't you realize that all of you together are the temple of God and that the Spirit of God lives in you? God will destroy anyone who destroys this temple. For God's temple is holy, and you are that temple.*

1 CORINTHIANS 6:12 | *You say, "I am allowed to do anything"— but not everything is good for you. And even though "I am allowed to do anything," I must not become a slave to anything.*

Your body was made to worship and glorify God and to fulfill the purpose for which he created you. When you do things that are not good for your body or that destroy your body, you are breaking down the very vessel God wants to use to help accomplish his work in the world. God works through people, which means he must work through your body, not just your spirit, to get things done.

How can my body be pure? I've done some pretty impure things.

PSALM 51:2, 7 | *Wash me clean from my guilt. Purify me from my sin. . . . Purify me from my sins, and I will be clean; wash me, and I will be whiter than snow.*

EPHESIANS 5:1, 3 | *Imitate God, therefore, in everything you do, because you are his dear children. . . . Let there be no sexual immorality, impurity, or greed among you. Such sins have no place among God's people.*

HEBREWS 10:22 | *Let us go right into the presence of God with sincere hearts fully trusting him. For our guilty consciences have been sprinkled with Christ's blood to make us clean, and our bodies have been washed with pure water.*

To have a pure body, you must start with a pure heart. God honors those who strive for pure hearts because it demonstrates a sincere commitment to be like Jesus. One of the most powerful truths Jesus taught is that when he forgives you, he sees you as pure and fully usable for his service, no matter what you have done. Now, forgiven and restored, strive as much as possible to avoid sin that violates God's intended plan for your body— sexual immorality, drunkenness, substance abuse, self-inflicted violence, and gluttony are among some of these sins.

Promise from God PSALM 24:3-5 | *Who may climb the mountain of the LORD? Who may stand in his holy place? Only those whose hands and hearts are pure. . . . They will receive the LORD's blessing and have a right relationship with God their savior.*

BOREDOM

Isn't being a Christian boring? Why do I get bored?

HEBREWS 6:11-12 | *Our great desire is that you will keep on loving others as long as life lasts, in order to make certain that what you hope for will come true. Then you will not become spiritually dull and indifferent. Instead, you will follow the example of those who are going to inherit God's promises because of their faith and endurance.*

Being a Christian can seem boring to many—"Don't do this," "You can't do that." But those who grasp what the Christian life is all about find it full and exciting. When you realize that almighty God wants to work through you to accomplish some of his work in the world, you will be amazed to see the great things he will accomplish through you. Focus on using and developing your God-given gifts, as well as on the eternal rewards God promises to believers, and your life will be continually exciting. If you become bored in your Christian life, it is because you are not making yourself available to God and asking him to pour his blessings onto others through you.

What eliminates boredom?

NEHEMIAH 8:10 | *The joy of the LORD is your strength!*

ROMANS 5:11 | *Now we can rejoice in our wonderful new relationship with God because our Lord Jesus Christ has made us friends of God.*

ROMANS 8:28 | *We know that God causes everything to work together for the good of those who love God and are called according to his purpose for them.*

God has a plan for you (see Jeremiah 29:11). Boredom disappears when you recognize his purpose for you. When you really try to follow Christ's example every day and ask God to do his work through you, you will never be bored!

Promise from God GALATIANS 6:9 | *Let's not get tired of doing what is good. At just the right time we will reap a harvest of blessing if we don't give up.*

CALL OF GOD

Has God called me to do specific things?

JEREMIAH 1:4-5 | *The LORD gave me this message: "I knew you before I formed you in your mother's womb. Before you were born I set you apart and appointed you as my prophet to the nations."*

God may call you to do a certain job or to accomplish a very specific task or ministry. When that happens, he will make sure you know what it is. You will feel a very strong sense of leading from him. It's up to you to respond and walk through the door of opportunity he opens.

ECCLESIASTES 11:9 | *Do everything you want to do; take it all in. But remember that you must give an account to God for everything you do.*

God gives you the freedom to follow many different roads over the course of your life and to pursue many different activities, but remember that you will have to answer to him for everything you do. Not everything you do is a call from God, but everything you do is accountable to God.

1 CORINTHIANS 12:4, 7 | *There are different kinds of spiritual gifts, but the same Spirit is the source of them all. . . . A spiritual gift is given to each of us so we can help each other.*

2 TIMOTHY 4:5 | *Work at telling others the Good News, and fully carry out the ministry God has given you.*

God gives each individual a spiritual gift (sometimes more than one!) and a special ministry in the church. You can use your gifts to help and encourage others and to bring glory to his name. These specific spiritual gifts help you fulfill the purpose for which God made you.

Promise from God 1 THESSALONIANS 5:23-24 | *May the God of peace make you holy in every way, and may your whole spirit and soul and body be kept blameless until our Lord Jesus Christ comes again. God will make this happen, for he who calls you is faithful.*

CHALLENGES

In a world that seems opposed to God, how do I handle the challenge of keeping my faith strong?

1 CHRONICLES 28:20 | *Be strong and courageous, and do the work. Don't be afraid or discouraged, for the LORD God . . . is with you. He will not fail you or forsake you.*

HEBREWS 6:18 | *God has given both his promise and his oath. These two things are unchangeable because it is impossible for God to lie. Therefore, we who have fled to him for refuge can have great confidence as we hold to the hope that lies before us.*

The strength to handle challenges comes from God, for he is all-powerful. Therefore you must stay close to him through Bible study and prayer, never doubting his promises to help and strengthen you. When you face opposition, always stand your ground on the truth of God's Word. When you do, you cannot be shaken.

What can I do when someone challenges me?

PROVERBS 15:31-32 | *If you listen to constructive criticism, you will be at home among the wise. If you reject discipline, you only harm yourself; but if you listen to correction, you grow in understanding.*

GALATIANS 2:11 | *[Paul said,] "When Peter came to Antioch, I had to oppose him to his face, for what he did was very wrong."*

When someone challenges sin in your life, you must humbly look inside yourself to determine whether or not the criticism is valid. You should be grateful to those who challenge you to live a godly life, but you also need to learn to discern when someone's challenge is not founded.

What if someone dares or challenges me to do wrong?

JOSHUA 1:7 | *Be strong and very courageous. Be careful to obey all the instructions Moses gave you. Do not deviate from them, turning either to the right or to the left. Then you will be successful in everything you do.*

2 CORINTHIANS 13:8 | *We cannot oppose the truth, but must always stand for the truth.*

Sin is often attractive and fun; otherwise it wouldn't tempt you. One of your greatest challenges is to do right in the face of such temptation, especially when it comes from friends.

How does God challenge me?

DEUTERONOMY 6:5 | *You must love the LORD your God with all your heart, all your soul, and all your strength.*

JOHN 14:15 | *[Jesus said,] "If you love me, obey my commandments."*

God challenges you to develop a relationship with him.

MARK 10:21 | *Looking at the man, Jesus felt genuine love for him. "There is still one thing you haven't done," he told him. "Go and sell all your possessions and give the money to the poor, and you will have treasure in heaven. Then come, follow me."*

God challenges you to examine your heart and make sure he has first place in your life.

JOHN 15:12-13 | *[Jesus said,] "This is my commandment: Love each other in the same way I have loved you. There is no greater love than to lay down one's life for one's friends."*

God challenges you to love others as much as he does.

2 TIMOTHY 3:16-17 | *All Scripture is inspired by God and is useful to teach us what is true and to make us realize what is wrong in our lives. It corrects us when we are wrong and teaches us to do what is right. God uses it to prepare and equip his people to do every good work.*

God challenges you to obey his Word, your blueprint for life.

Promise from God PSALM 37:5 | *Commit everything you do to the LORD. Trust him, and he will help you.*

CHARACTER

I want to have good character, but some of my friends laugh at me for my clean living. What should I do?

1 CORINTHIANS 15:32-33 | *"Let's feast and drink, for tomorrow we die!" Don't be fooled by those who say such things, for "bad company corrupts good character."*

If your friends' influence keeps you from having good character, the answer is to get different friends who will respect your godly values. That doesn't mean your only friends should be Christians, but it does mean that real friends will respect your beliefs. Peer pressure is one way your character is tested. God promises that you will not be tested beyond what you can handle with his help (see 1 Corinthians 10:13).

Why does building character have to be so hard?

PSALM 105:19 | *Until the time came to fulfill his dreams, the LORD tested Joseph's character.*

ROMANS 5:4 | *Endurance develops strength of character, and character strengthens our confident hope of salvation.*

One of the basic principles of life is that adversity produces strength. Your muscles grow only when stretched to their limit. Your character grows only when pressure pushes against it and tests its strength. Developing strong character, therefore, is a process that takes time and constant attention.

What attributes are found in godly character?

GALATIANS 5:22-23 | *The Holy Spirit produces this kind of fruit in our lives: love, joy, peace, patience, kindness, goodness, faithfulness, gentleness, and self-control.*

The fruit of the Spirit—love, joy, peace, patience, kindness, goodness, faithfulness, gentleness, and self-control—are some of the essential traits of godly character.

MICAH 6:8 | *O people, the LORD has told you what is good, and this is what he requires of you: to do what is right, to love mercy, and to walk humbly with your God.*

Justice, righteousness, mercy, and humility are essential traits of godly character.

How can I develop character?

DEUTERONOMY 8:2 | *Remember how the LORD your God led you through the wilderness for these forty years, humbling you and testing you to prove your character, and to find out whether or not you would obey his commands.*

JAMES 1:4 | *When your endurance is fully developed, you will be perfect and complete, needing nothing.*

You are not born with godly character; it is developed through experience—by facing daily challenges and choosing wisely, by overcoming tests of adversity, by resisting temptation, and by committing daily to knowing God better through prayer, Bible reading, and good teaching.

PHILIPPIANS 1:9 | *I pray that your love will overflow more and more, and that you will keep on growing in knowledge and understanding.*

1 PETER 4:19 | *Keep on doing what is right, and trust your lives to the God who created you, for he will never fail you.*

Developing character is like developing anything else: You must practice. Keep on doing what is good and right, and constantly practice character traits such as kindness, generosity, compassion, and honesty. What you value most is usually what you will work hardest to attain.

Promise from God GALATIANS 5:22-23 | *The Holy Spirit produces this kind of fruit in our lives: love, joy, peace, patience, kindness, goodness, faithfulness, gentleness, and self-control.*

CHEATING

Why does cheating, on a large or a small scale, matter to God?

PROVERBS 11:1 | *The LORD detests the use of dishonest scales, but he delights in accurate weights.*

Cheating is the opposite of honesty, because the motives behind cheating are always to deceive someone else. How can anyone trust a cheater?

LUKE 16:10 | *If you are faithful in little things, you will be faithful in large ones. But if you are dishonest in little things, you won't be honest with greater responsibilities.*

Character is tested in the small choices you make. A little bit of cheating is cut out of the same piece of cloth as cheating on a large scale. Just as a small drop of red dye colors a large glass of clear water, a small act of deception colors your character.

ROMANS 13:9-10 | *The commandments say, "You must not commit adultery. You must not murder. You must not steal. You must not covet." These . . . are summed up in this one commandment: "Love your neighbor as yourself." Love does no wrong to others, so love fulfills the requirements of God's law.*

Cheating is evidence that you do not love or respect the person you cheated and that you are thinking only of yourself.

How do I cheat God?

MALACHI 3:8 | *Should people cheat God? Yet you have cheated me! But you ask, "What do you mean? When did we ever cheat you?" You have cheated me of the tithes and offerings due to me.*

You cheat God when you do not give to him what he deserves of your time, your money, your service, or your heart.

Promise from God PSALM 32:2 | *What joy for those whose record the LORD has cleared of guilt, whose lives are lived in complete honesty!*

CHOICES

How do I know whether I am making good or bad choices?

GENESIS 13:10-13 | *Lot took a long look at the fertile plains of the Jordan Valley in the direction of Zoar. The whole area was well watered everywhere. . . . Lot chose for himself the whole Jordan Valley to the east of [him]. . . . Lot moved his tents to a place near Sodom and settled among the cities of the plain. But the people of this area were extremely wicked and constantly sinned against the LORD.*

GENESIS 25:30-31, 33-34 | *Esau said to Jacob, "I'm starved! Give me some of that red stew!" . . . "All right," Jacob replied, "but trade me your rights as the firstborn son." . . . So Esau swore an oath, thereby selling all his rights as the firstborn to his brother, Jacob. Then Jacob gave Esau some bread and lentil stew. Esau ate the meal, then got up and left. He showed contempt for his rights as the firstborn.*

If your choices are being guided primarily by selfish ambition or a desire for physical fulfillment, it is very likely that you are making bad choices, like Lot and Esau did.

1 KINGS 12:8 | *Rehoboam rejected the advice of the older men and instead asked the opinion of the young men who had grown up with him and were now his advisers.*

PROVERBS 12:15 | *Fools think their own way is right, but the wise listen to others.*

If you reject the advice of proven wise counselors, like Rehoboam did, you are probably making a foolish choice.

But if you listen to advice and weigh it carefully, you are more likely to make good choices.

PROVERBS 1:7 | *Fear of the LORD is the foundation of true knowledge, but fools despise wisdom and discipline.*

If your decisions are being guided by reverence for God and by a desire for his wisdom, then you are on your way to making good choices.

JOHN 5:19 | *Jesus explained, "I tell you the truth, the Son can do nothing by himself. He does only what he sees the Father doing."*

If you, like Jesus, keep in mind what God would have you do, then you are more likely to make choices that will honor him.

GALATIANS 5:22-23 | *The Holy Spirit produces this kind of fruit in our lives: love, joy, peace, patience, kindness, goodness, faithfulness, gentleness, and self-control. There is no law against these things!*

When you make the choice to follow the Holy Spirit's leading, the fruits of the Spirit are produced in your life, while bad choices often involve rejecting his influence in your heart.

Promise from God PSALM 23:3 | *He guides me along right paths, bringing honor to his name.*

CHURCH

Why should I be involved in church?

PSALM 27:4 | *The one thing I ask of the LORD—the thing I seek most—is to live in the house of the LORD all the days of my life, delighting in the LORD's perfections and meditating in his Temple.*

PSALM 84:4 | *What joy for those who can live in your house, always singing your praises.*

Even though God lives in the heart of every believer, he also lives in the community of the church. When the church is gathered together, God is there in a special way.

EPHESIANS 2:19-22 | *You Gentiles are no longer strangers and foreigners. You are citizens along with all of God's holy people. You are members of God's family. Together, we are his house, built on the foundation of the apostles and the prophets. And the cornerstone is Christ Jesus himself. We are carefully joined together in him, becoming a holy temple for the Lord. Through him you Gentiles are also being made part of this dwelling where God lives by his Spirit.*

All believers together form God's family and are joined together. But only by meeting with other believers can you experience this reality.

HEBREWS 10:25 | *Let us not neglect our meeting together, as some people do, but encourage one another, especially now that the day of his return is drawing near.*

Good friends are a wonderful gift, but fellowship at church among other believers is unique, because the living God is in your midst. The church brings people together who have a common perspective on life. Christian fellowship provides a place of honest sharing about the things that really matter, encouragement to stay strong in the face of temptation and persecution, and unique wisdom to deal with problems.

How are the members of the body of Christ—the church—supposed to function together?

ROMANS 12:4-6 | *Just as our bodies have many parts and each part has a special function, so it is with Christ's body. We are many parts of one body, and we all belong to each other. In his grace, God has given us different gifts for doing certain things well.*

EPHESIANS 4:16 | *He makes the whole body fit together perfectly. As each part does its own special work, it helps the other parts grow, so that the whole body is healthy and growing and full of love.*

God intends the different members of the body to find their places and to function in their areas of ministry so that the body as a whole can be spiritually healthy.

EPHESIANS 4:3-6 | *Make every effort to keep yourselves united in the Spirit, binding yourselves together with peace. For there is one body and one Spirit, just as you have been called to one glorious hope for the future. There is one Lord, one faith, one baptism, and one God and Father, who is over all and in all and living through all.*

God especially desires unity and peace in the church because this shows the world how people of different interests and backgrounds, as they rely on the Holy Spirit, can work together for a common purpose.

Promise from God MATTHEW 16:18 | *[Jesus said,] "Upon this rock I will build my church, and all the powers of hell will not conquer it."*

COMMUNICATION

How does God communicate with me?

2 TIMOTHY 3:16-17 | *All Scripture is inspired by God and is useful to teach us what is true and to make us realize what is wrong in our lives. It corrects us when we are wrong and teaches us to do what is right. God uses it to prepare and equip his people to do every good work.*

God communicates with you through his Word, the Bible. Read it daily to keep in touch with him.

JOHN 1:14 | *The Word became human and made his home among us. He was full of unfailing love and faithfulness. And we have seen his glory, the glory of the Father's one and only Son.*

HEBREWS 1:1-2 | *Long ago God spoke many times and in many ways to our ancestors through the prophets. And now in these final days, he has spoken to us through his Son.*

God communicates with you through his Son, Jesus Christ. He revealed who God is and what God is like as he walked on this earth two thousand years ago.

JOHN 14:26 | *When the Father sends the Advocate as my representative—that is, the Holy Spirit—he will teach you everything and will remind you of everything I have told you.*

ROMANS 8:16 | *His Spirit joins with our spirit to affirm that we are God's children.*

God communicates with you through his Holy Spirit.
Pay special attention to the way he speaks to your heart
and spirit.

ROMANS 2:14-15 | *Even Gentiles, who do not have God's
written law, show that they know his law when they instinc-
tively obey it, even without having heard it. They demonstrate that God's law is written in their hearts, for their own
conscience and thoughts either accuse them or tell them they
are doing right.*

God communicates with you through your conscience,
which is your God-given, internal radar to help you know
right from wrong. Always listen to your conscience. If you
neglect it, it will become dull and eventually you will no
longer hear it.

PSALM 19:1-2 | *The heavens proclaim the glory of God. The skies
display his craftsmanship. Day after day they continue to speak;
night after night they make him known.*

ROMANS 1:19-20 | *They know the truth about God because he has
made it obvious to them. For ever since the world was created,
people have seen the earth and sky. Through everything God
made, they can clearly see his invisible qualities—his eternal
power and divine nature. So they have no excuse for not
knowing God.*

God communicates with you through his creation. All nature
sings about a majestic God who created the starry heavens,
the roar of thunder, and the glorious snowcapped mountains.
But nature also whispers about God's mind-boggling attention to detail in the wings of a butterfly, the variety of plants,
and the complexity of a strand of DNA.

1 SAMUEL 3:7-10 | *Samuel did not yet know the LORD because he had never had a message from the LORD before. So the LORD called a third time, and once more Samuel got up and went to Eli. "Here I am. Did you call me?" Then Eli realized it was the LORD who was calling the boy. So he said to Samuel, "Go and lie down again, and if someone calls again, say, 'Speak, LORD, your servant is listening.'" So Samuel went back to bed. And the LORD came and called as before, "Samuel! Samuel!" And Samuel replied, "Speak, your servant is listening."*

ISAIAH 45:2, 4 | *This is what the LORD says: "I will go before you, Cyrus. . . . And why have I called you for this work? Why did I call you by name when you did not know me? It is for the sake of . . . Israel my chosen one."*

God communicates with you through other people. Mostly, he uses godly people to give you spiritual advice and help you mature in your faith. But sometimes he uses people who don't even know him to unwittingly communicate his truth to you.

Promise from God JOHN 10:27 | *My sheep listen to my voice; I know them, and they follow me.*

COMPARISONS

What are the dangers of comparing myself to others?

JOHN 21:21-22 | *Peter asked Jesus, "What about him, Lord?" Jesus replied, "If I want him to remain alive until I return, what is that to you? As for you, follow me."*

Comparing yourself to someone else takes your focus off Jesus.

1 SAMUEL 8:19-20 | *"We still want a king," [the people of Israel] said. "We want to be like the nations around us."*

Comparing what you have with what someone else has may cause you to miss enjoying what God has already given you.

LUKE 18:11, 13-14 | *The Pharisee stood by himself and prayed this prayer: "I thank you, God, that I am not a sinner like everyone else." . . . But the tax collector stood at a distance and dared not even lift his eyes to heaven as he prayed . . . "O God, be merciful to me, for I am a sinner." [Jesus said,] "I tell you, this sinner, not the Pharisee, returned home justified before God. For those who exalt themselves will be humbled, and those who humble themselves will be exalted."*

Comparing the condition of your heart to that of someone else can lead to false righteousness, arrogance, and pride. On the flip side, thinking you are far worse than others can lead to shame, discouragement, and despair. God knows the real condition of your heart, and he loves you as you are. Keep focused on him and you won't have a need to compare.

1 SAMUEL 18:7-11 | *This was their song: "Saul has killed his thousands, and David his ten thousands!" This made Saul very angry. "What's this?" he said. "They credit David with ten thousands and me with only thousands. Next they'll be making him their king!" So from that time on Saul kept a jealous eye on David. The very next day . . . Saul had a spear in his hand, and he suddenly hurled it at David.*

Comparing yourself to someone else can lead to jealousy, which leads to anger, and eventually to harmful behavior. Saul's jealousy so consumed him that he tried to kill David.

How can I avoid the dangers of comparing myself to others?

ROMANS 14:10, 12 | *Why do you condemn another believer? Why do you look down on another believer? Remember, we will all stand before the judgment seat of God. . . . Yes, each of us will give a personal account to God.*

When judging people, God uses his own standards. He does not judge you in comparison to what others have accomplished but in comparison to his standards of love and right living. Set God and his commandments as your standards of comparison.

GALATIANS 6:4-5 | *Pay careful attention to your own work, for then you will get the satisfaction of a job well done, and you won't need to compare yourself to anyone else. For we are each responsible for our own conduct.*

Examine your own faith and actions. Where is your heart with God? Are you living by Jesus' words? Are you doing what you should? Are you finding satisfaction in doing your work well? If so, you have no need to compare yourself to others.

ROMANS 12:15 | *Be happy with those who are happy, and weep with those who weep.*

Rejoice with others in their successes; don't wish their success was yours. This is much easier to do when you're not comparing yourself to them.

Promise from God ISAIAH 40:25, 28 | *"To whom will you compare me? Who is my equal?" asks the Holy One. . . . No one can measure the depths of his understanding.*

COMPETITION

Is competition good or bad?

1 CORINTHIANS 9:24 | *Don't you realize that in a race everyone runs, but only one person gets the prize? So run to win!*

1 CORINTHIANS 15:10 | *Whatever I am now, it is all because God poured out his special favor on me—and not without results. For I have worked harder than any of the other apostles; yet it was not I but God who was working through me by his grace.*

Competition can drive you to improve yourself personally and to sharpen your skills. Paul is a good example of a competitive person whom God used to reach people with the good news about Jesus and to plant churches throughout the world.

When does competition become a bad thing?

2 TIMOTHY 2:5 | *Athletes cannot win the prize unless they follow the rules.*

Competition can be unhealthy when it causes you to sin by trying to win at all costs. When winning is everything, you almost always compromise your integrity.

GENESIS 4:4-5, 8 | *The LORD accepted Abel and his gift, but he did not accept Cain and his gift. This made Cain very angry, and he looked dejected. . . . One day Cain suggested to his brother, "Let's go out into the fields." And while they were in the field, Cain attacked his brother, Abel, and killed him.*

Competition can lead to jealousy, anger, and bitterness if your sole focus is beating those you are competing against rather than the larger goal of what you are trying to achieve.

MATTHEW 18:1-4 | *The disciples came to Jesus and asked, "Who is greatest in the Kingdom of Heaven?" Jesus called a little child to him and put the child among them. Then he said, "I tell you the truth, unless you turn from your sins and become like little children, you will never get into the Kingdom of Heaven. So anyone who becomes as humble as this little child is the greatest in the Kingdom of Heaven."*

Competition can be a foothold for pride and jealousy because it can lead you to compare yourself with others. Everyone has equal worth in God's eyes, and anytime you begin to think of yourself as more important or better than others, your competitive spirit is taking you in the wrong direction. When humility fuels your competitive nature, you give everything you have to doing your best rather than besting others.

Promise from God 1 CORINTHIANS 15:57 | *Thank God! He gives us victory over sin and death through our Lord Jesus Christ.*

COMPLAINING

What should I do instead of complaining?

PHILIPPIANS 2:14-15 | *Do everything without complaining and arguing, so that no one can criticize you. Live clean, innocent lives as children of God, shining like bright lights in a world full of crooked and perverse people.*

Instead of complaining about others, say something nice about them. If you can't do that, then don't say anything at all. At least if you're quiet, you can't be blamed for being negative or critical.

LAMENTATIONS 3:39-40 | *Why should we, mere humans, complain when we are punished for our sins? Instead, let us test and examine our ways. Let us turn back to the LORD.*

Instead of complaining when you are punished for your sins, repent of your sins and thank God he has promised to forgive them.

LUKE 6:37 | *Do not judge others, and you will not be judged. Do not condemn others, or it will all come back against you. Forgive others, and you will be forgiven.*

Instead of complaining about the mistakes of others, forgive them as you would like to be forgiven.

How should I react when someone complains about me?

PROVERBS 15:31-32 | *If you listen to constructive criticism, you will be at home among the wise. If you reject discipline, you only harm yourself; but if you listen to correction, you grow in understanding.*

PROVERBS 25:12 | *To one who listens, valid criticism is like a gold earring or other gold jewelry.*

PROVERBS 29:1 | *Whoever stubbornly refuses to accept criticism will suddenly be destroyed beyond recovery.*

Ask yourself if the person is complaining about you or trying to offer you constructive criticism. Constructive criticism should always be welcomed, especially if it is given in a spirit of love. You should always listen to criticism and try to learn and grow from it.

What is it about complaining that is so wrong?

NUMBERS 11:1 | *The people began to complain about their hardship, and the LORD heard everything they said. Then the LORD's anger blazed against them, and he sent a fire to rage among them, and he destroyed some of the people in the outskirts of the camp.*

God considers complaining a sin because it demonstrates an attitude of ungratefulness.

DEUTERONOMY 6:16 | *You must not test the LORD your God as you did when you complained at Massah.*

Complaining is often a form of criticizing God and others, and it tests everyone's patience. Complaining focuses on what you don't have rather than on what you do have. It is offensive to God because you are ignoring all he has already blessed you with instead of being grateful for it.

JOB 10:1 | *I am disgusted with my life. Let me complain freely. My bitter soul must complain.*

Complaining often reveals an attitude of bitterness.

JAMES 4:11 | *Don't speak evil against each other, dear brothers and sisters. If you criticize and judge each other, then you are criticizing and judging God's law. But your job is to obey the law, not to judge whether it applies to you.*

Complaining about others usually leads you to say things about them you may later regret. It often leads to gossip and slander.

Promise from God EPHESIANS 4:29 | *Let everything you say be good and helpful, so that your words will be an encouragement to those who hear them.*

COMPROMISE

When is compromise appropriate?

ROMANS 14:15 | *If another believer is distressed by what you eat, you are not acting in love if you eat it. Don't let your eating ruin someone for whom Christ died.*

ROMANS 15:1 | *We who are strong must be considerate of those who are sensitive. . . . We must not just please ourselves.*

Sometimes you must compromise so you don't offend others or cause them to stumble in their faith.

PHILIPPIANS 2:2 | *Make me truly happy by agreeing wholeheartedly with each other, loving one another, and working together with one mind and purpose.*

Sometimes you need to compromise for the sake of unity in the church. Agreement may mean giving up something you want for the sake of what is best for all. It's okay to compromise your personal preferences—but never essential Christian beliefs.

How do I live in today's culture without compromising my convictions?

DANIEL 1:8, 12-14 | *Daniel was determined not to defile himself by eating the food and wine given to them by the king. He asked the chief of staff for permission not to eat these unacceptable foods . . . "Please test us for ten days on a diet of vegetables and water," Daniel said. "At the end of the ten days, see how we look compared to the other young men who are eating the king's food. Then make your decision in light of what you see." The attendant agreed to Daniel's suggestion and tested them for ten days.*

Never be afraid to take a stand for what you know is right and true, but do so in a respectful, humble manner. You may be surprised how often you will be admired for sticking to your beliefs, even if others disagree with them. But even if you meet resistance, you must not compromise by going against God's Word.

EXODUS 34:12 | *Be very careful never to make a treaty with the people who live in the land where you are going. If you do, you will follow their evil ways and be trapped.*

HEBREWS 3:12-13 | *Be careful then, dear brothers and sisters. Make sure that your own hearts are not evil and unbelieving, turning you away from the living God. You must warn each other every day, while it is still "today," so that none of you will be deceived by sin and hardened against God.*

You must always be on the alert when living or working with those who don't see sin as something wrong. You can easily find yourself compromising and agreeing to commit "little" sins. This will eventually dull your sensitivity to other sins. A "little" sin now and then can lead to a life defined by sin.

JUDGES 16:15-17 | *Delilah pouted, "How can you tell me, 'I love you,' when you don't share your secrets with me? . . . You still haven't told me what makes you so strong!" She tormented him with her nagging day after day until he was sick to death of it. Finally, Samson shared his secret with her.*

You are most likely to compromise in areas where you are spiritually weak. Learn to recognize where you are vulnerable so that you are strong enough to resist when the temptation to compromise comes.

Promise from God 1 CORINTHIANS 10:13 | *God is faithful. He will not allow the temptation to be more than you can stand. When you are tempted, he will show you a way out so that you can endure.*

CONFESSION

Does God truly forgive my sin when I confess it to him?

PSALM 32:5 | *Finally, I confessed all my sins to you and stopped trying to hide my guilt. I said to myself, "I will confess my rebellion to the LORD." And you forgave me! All my guilt is gone.*

1 JOHN 1:9 | *If we confess our sins to him, he is faithful and just to forgive us.*

Confession is the act of recognizing and admitting sin to God so he can forgive you and indicates your desire to have your sins forgiven. If you have no desire to have your sins forgiven, God will not force his forgiveness on you. However, when you sincerely confess your sins to God, he fully forgives you.

PROVERBS 28:13 | *People who conceal their sins will not prosper, but if they confess and turn from them, they will receive mercy.*

Confession paves the way for God to work in you. It wipes the slate clean so that you can be reconciled to God and have another chance to live for him.

Promise from God 1 JOHN 1:9 | *If we confess our sins to him, he is faithful and just to forgive us our sins and to cleanse us.*

CONFLICT

What causes conflict?

2 SAMUEL 15:6, 12 | *Absalom . . . stole the hearts of all the people . . . , and the conspiracy gained momentum.*

JAMES 4:2 | *You want what you don't have, so you scheme and kill to get it. You are jealous of what others have, but you can't get it, so you fight and wage war to take it away from them.*

Conflict begins when a person, group, or nation isn't getting what it wants and confronts whoever or whatever is the obstacle to try to get it. On a personal level, you want someone's behavior to be different, you want your way on some issue, you want to win, you want some possession, you want someone's loyalty. The list can go on and on. When another person isn't willing to give you what you want, you find yourself in conflict. Unresolved conflict can sometimes lead to open warfare.

ACTS 15:37-39 | *Barnabas . . . wanted to take along John Mark. But Paul disagreed strongly. . . . Their disagreement was so sharp that they separated.*

Conflict begins when people with opposing viewpoints are not willing to find common ground.

ESTHER 3:2, 5-6 | *Mordecai refused to bow. . . . [Haman] was filled with rage . . . so he decided it was not enough to lay hands on Mordecai alone. . . . He looked for a way to destroy all the Jews throughout the entire empire.*

Conflict begins when your pride is hurt and you want to strike back.

How do I keep conflict with others to a minimum?

PROVERBS 26:17 | *Interfering in someone else's argument is as foolish as yanking a dog's ears.*

It is sometimes tempting to step into someone else's argument to help "solve it," but doing so often only makes it worse.

ROMANS 12:18 | *Do all that you can to live in peace with everyone.*

As Christ's ambassador, you need to work actively to be at peace with others.

EPHESIANS 4:3 | *Make every effort to keep yourselves united in the Spirit, binding yourselves together with peace.*

Living in close fellowship with God through the Holy Spirit will help you to bring unity and peace to your relationships.

What are some ways to resolve conflict?

GENESIS 13:8-9 | *Abram said to Lot, "Let's not allow this conflict to come between us or our herdsmen. After all, we are close relatives! The whole countryside is open to you. Take your choice of any section of the land you want, and we will separate. If you want the land to the left, then I'll take the land on the right. If you prefer the land on the right, then I'll go to the left."*

1 CORINTHIANS 6:7 | *Even to have such lawsuits with one another is a defeat for you. Why not just accept the injustice and leave it at that? Why not let yourselves be cheated?*

Solving conflict takes initiative; someone must make the first move. Abram gave Lot first choice, putting family peace above personal desires. Like Abram, you might have to give up what you want in order to resolve a conflict over personal interests.

2 TIMOTHY 2:24-25 | *A servant of the Lord must not quarrel but must be kind to everyone, be able to teach, and be patient with difficult people. Gently instruct those who oppose the truth.*

When someone disagrees with what you are saying, maintain a gracious, gentle, and patient attitude instead of becoming angry and defensive.

Can I hope to resolve conflict with an enemy?

MATTHEW 5:43-45 | *[Jesus said,] "You have heard the law that says, 'Love your neighbor' and hate your enemy. But I say, love your enemies! Pray for those who persecute you! In that way, you will be acting as true children of your Father in heaven."*

Human nature wants to love friends and hate enemies. But Jesus brought a new order that adds a divine perspective—the only way to resolve some conflicts is to reach out in love to your enemy. This kind of love has sometimes eliminated enemies by turning them into friends.

Promise from God PSALM 55:18 | *He ransoms me and keeps me safe from the battle waged against me, though many still oppose me.*

CONSCIENCE

Where does my conscience come from?

ROMANS 1:19-20 | *[People] know the truth about God because he has made it obvious to them. For ever since the world was created, people have seen the earth and sky. Through everything God made, they can clearly see his invisible qualities—his eternal power and divine nature. So they have no excuse for not knowing God.*

Conscience is the God-given instinct he put deep inside you that guides you to know right from wrong. It is the part of you that helps you understand if you are in line with God's will and God's Word.

If God created everyone with a conscience, why have I done such horrible things?

1 TIMOTHY 1:19 | *Cling to your faith in Christ, and keep your conscience clear. For some people have deliberately violated their consciences; as a result, their faith has been shipwrecked.*

Sin is the act of going against your conscience. You know what you are doing is wrong because your conscience tells you so, but you do it anyway because it is so appealing. If you consistently go against what your conscience tells you, you can train yourself not to hear it calling out to you, warning you of danger. Without a strong conscience, you can become insensitive to sin.

How do I keep a clear conscience?

ACTS 24:16 | *I always try to maintain a clear conscience before God and all people.*

Keeping a clear and sharp conscience is the best way to keep away from sin. But keeping away from sin is also the best way to keep a clear conscience. When you sin, your conscience has a reason to witness against you. When you avoid sin, you are actively nurturing your conscience and keeping it from witnessing against you.

Promise from God PSALM 119:105 | *Your word is a lamp to guide my feet and a light for my path.*

CONSEQUENCES

Does sin always have negative consequences?

ISAIAH 30:12-13 | *This is the reply of the Holy One of Israel: "Because you despise what I tell you and trust instead in oppression and lies, calamity will come upon you suddenly— like a bulging wall that bursts and falls. In an instant it will collapse and come crashing down."*

GALATIANS 6:7 | *Don't be misled—you cannot mock the justice of God. You will always harvest what you plant.*

It may seem for a time that your sin does not have negative consequences, but they always come, sooner or later.

1 CORINTHIANS 3:13-15 | *On the judgment day, fire will reveal what kind of work each builder has done. The fire will show if a person's work has any value. If the work survives, that builder will receive a reward. But if the work is burned up, the builder will suffer great loss. The builder will be saved, but like someone barely escaping through a wall of flames.*

Some of the consequences of sin will not be felt until the Day of Judgment. Even those who have salvation through Jesus Christ will receive fewer or more rewards based on the consequences of their actions.

GALATIANS 6:8 | *Those who live only to satisfy their own sinful nature will harvest decay and death from that sinful nature. But those who live to please the Spirit will harvest everlasting life from the Spirit.*

Sin always has negative consequences, but the reverse is also true: Living to please God always has positive consequences.

Can forgiveness of sin stop sin's consequences?

2 SAMUEL 12:13-14 | *David confessed to Nathan, "I have sinned against the LORD." Nathan replied, "Yes, but the LORD has forgiven you, and you won't die for this sin. Nevertheless . . . your child will die."*

The consequences of sin are often irreversible. When God forgives you, he doesn't necessarily eliminate the consequences of your wrongdoing. He allows the natural consequences of your actions to happen. These consequences should be a powerful reminder for you when you face temptation again.

Can there also be positive consequences to my actions?

JEREMIAH 17:7 | *Blessed are those who trust in the LORD and have made the LORD their hope and confidence.*

A life focused on God brings joy to God and many blessings to you. The more you trust and obey God, the more you will experience the blessings he gives.

HEBREWS 11:6 | *It is impossible to please God without faith. Anyone who wants to come to him must believe that God exists and that he rewards those who sincerely seek him.*

Looking for God brings the reward of experiencing his presence.

Promise from God ROMANS 6:23 | *The wages of sin is death, but the free gift of God is eternal life through Christ Jesus our Lord.*

CONSISTENCY

How do I develop more consistency in my walk with God?

JOHN 14:15 | *[Jesus said,] "If you love me, obey my commandments."*

Practice. Work toward conscious obedience.

MICAH 6:8 | *O people, the LORD has told you what is good, and this is what he requires of you: to do what is right, to love mercy, and to walk humbly with your God.*

JOHN 15:10-11 | *[Jesus said,] "When you obey my commandments, you remain in my love. . . . I have told you these things so that you will be filled with my joy. Yes, your joy will overflow!"*

Develop a desire to obey God. If you have observed children, you know they usually try to obey because they want to please their parents, even if they don't always achieve it. That is what God is looking for. He knows that because of your sinful nature, you won't always obey him. What he wants is your desire to obey, because that is the sign that you love and respect him, that you believe his way for you is best. If you consistently disobey because you enjoy it, you do not love God.

1 PETER 4:19 | *Keep on doing what is right, and trust your lives to the God who created you.*

When you drift away from consistent obedience to God, you lose your eternal perspective of why obedience is so important. Your daily choices become more selfish, and you will slide into being cynical and dissatisfied with your life.

Promise from God 1 PETER 4:19 | *Keep on doing what is right, and trust your lives to the God who created you, for he will never fail you.*

CONVICTIONS

What are some basic convictions I must have to live out my faith effectively?

EXODUS 20:2-3 | *"I am the LORD your God, who rescued you from the land of Egypt, the place of your slavery. You must not have any other god but me."*

Accept that God must have first priority in your life.

COLOSSIANS 1:23 | *You must continue to believe this truth and stand firmly in it. Don't drift away from the assurance you received when you heard the Good News.*

2 TIMOTHY 3:16 | *All Scripture is inspired by God and is useful to teach us what is true and to make us realize what is wrong in our lives. It corrects us when we are wrong and teaches us to do what is right.*

Believe that the Bible was written by God and is God's truth for all matters of faith and life.

ROMANS 4:21 | *He was fully convinced that God is able to do whatever he promises.*

Be assured that God always keeps his promises.

HEBREWS 11:1 | *Faith is the confidence that what we hope for will actually happen; it gives us assurance about things we cannot see.*

Have confidence in God. You can't see faith, but you can see the evidence of faith as God does his supernatural work through people. This gives you assurance that your faith is real and a conviction that one day you will see what you can't now.

ROMANS 10:9 | *If you confess with your mouth that Jesus is Lord and believe in your heart that God raised him from the dead, you will be saved.*

2 CORINTHIANS 5:17 | *Anyone who belongs to Christ has become a new person. The old life is gone; a new life has begun!*

1 JOHN 1:9 | *If we confess our sins to him, he is faithful and just to forgive us our sins and to cleanse us from all wickedness.*

Accept that salvation is of God. If you are truly sorry for your sins and confess them to God (repentance) and if you believe that God's Son, Jesus, died for you, taking upon himself the punishment for sin you deserve, then God forgives you and gives you the gift of salvation. The moment this happens, the Holy Spirit enters your life and begins transforming you into a new person on the inside. Then you know that your life can and will be different.

PSALM 17:6 | *I am praying to you because I know you will answer, O God. Bend down and listen as I pray.*

Believe that God answers prayer.

EPHESIANS 4:15 | *We will speak the truth in love, growing in every way more and more like Christ, who is the head of his body, the church.*

If you live by the truths in God's Word, you will become more and more like Jesus, which is your primary goal.

ROMANS 8:39 | *No power in the sky above or in the earth below—indeed, nothing in all creation will ever be able to separate us from the love of God that is revealed in Christ Jesus our Lord.*

Know that nothing can separate you from God's love for you.

1 PETER 1:21 | *Through Christ you have come to trust in God. And you have placed your faith and hope in God because he raised Christ from the dead and gave him great glory.*

Remember that Christ has power over death, for he brought himself back from the dead.

PSALM 135:5 | *I know the greatness of the LORD—that our Lord is greater than any other god.*

Rest in the knowledge that no one is greater than God. He is sovereign and all-powerful.

How do I live out my convictions?

PSALM 119:7 | *As I learn your righteous regulations, I will thank you by living as I should!*

PSALM 143:8 | *Let me hear of your unfailing love each morning, for I am trusting you. Show me where to walk, for I give myself to you.*

You live out your convictions by making daily decisions to obey God's Word, the standard for your convictions.

DANIEL 3:16-18 | *Shadrach, Meshach, and Abednego replied, "O Nebuchadnezzar, we do not need to defend ourselves before you. If we are thrown into the blazing furnace, the God whom we serve is able to save us. . . . But even if he doesn't, we want to make it clear to you, Your Majesty, that we will never serve your gods or worship the gold statue you have set up."*

You live out your convictions by not compromising your conscience and by keeping God your main focus.

DANIEL 1:8 | *Daniel was determined not to defile himself by eating the food and wine given to [him] by the king. He asked the chief of staff for permission not to eat these unacceptable foods.*

You live out your convictions by respectfully negotiating issues with others without compromising your values.

1 THESSALONIANS 2:2 | *You know how badly we had been treated at Philippi just before we came to you and how much we suffered there. Yet our God gave us the courage to declare his Good News to you boldly, in spite of great opposition.*

You live out your convictions by asking God for courage.

2 CORINTHIANS 4:13 | *We continue to preach because we have the same kind of faith the psalmist had when he said, "I believed in God, so I spoke."*

You live out your convictions by having faith that God is real and his message in the Bible is true.

Promise from God ROMANS 2:7 | *He will give eternal life to those who keep on doing good, seeking after the glory and honor and immortality that God offers.*

COOPERATION

Why should I cooperate with those I don't get along with?

EXODUS 17:11-13 | *As long as Moses held up the staff in his hand, the Israelites had the advantage. But whenever he dropped his hand, the Amalekites gained the advantage. Moses' arms soon became so tired he could no longer hold them up. So Aaron and Hur found a stone for him to sit on. Then they stood on each side of Moses, holding up his hands. So his hands held steady until sunset. As a result, Joshua overwhelmed the army of Amalek in battle.*

Moses and Aaron did not always see eye to eye, but in this instance of cooperation, the result was a decisive win for the Israelites. When you cooperate with others, God can accomplish remarkable things through you.

PROVERBS 27:17 | *As iron sharpens iron, so a friend sharpens a friend.*

Disagreements can produce positive results—they can introduce new ideas that may challenge and stimulate your thinking.

1 CORINTHIANS 1:10 | *I appeal to you, dear brothers and sisters, by the authority of our Lord Jesus Christ, to live in harmony with each other. Let there be no divisions in the church. Rather, be of one mind, united in thought and purpose.*

Loving confrontation is different from argumentativeness. Conflict is inevitable. When it arises, true cooperation seeks the highest good for all.

Promise from God PSALM 133:1 | *How wonderful and pleasant it is when brothers live together in harmony!*

COURAGE

Where do I get the courage to go on when life seems too hard or obstacles seem too big?

JOSHUA 1:9 | *This is my command—be strong and courageous! Do not be afraid or discouraged. For the LORD your God is with you wherever you go.*

ISAIAH 41:10 | *Don't be afraid, for I am with you. Don't be discouraged, for I am your God. I will strengthen you and help you. I will hold you up with my victorious right hand.*

Courage is not misplaced confidence in your own strength, but well-placed confidence in God's strength. Throughout your life you will find yourself in scary situations—mortal danger, extreme stress, major illness, money issues, or any number of problems. True courage comes from understanding that God is stronger than your biggest problem or strongest enemy and from knowing that he wants you to use his power to help you.

How do I find the courage to face change?

GENESIS 46:3 | *"I am God. . . . Do not be afraid to go down to Egypt, for there I will make your family into a great nation."*

Change may be part of God's plan for you. If so, what you are headed into will give you joy and satisfaction beyond your expectations. Remember, the greatest advances in life come through change.

EXODUS 4:13 | *Moses again pleaded, "Lord, please! Send anyone else."*

To experience fear is normal. To be paralyzed by fear, however, can be an indication that you doubt God's ability to care for you in the face of change.

2 SAMUEL 4:1 | *When Ishbosheth, Saul's son, heard about Abner's death at Hebron, he lost all courage, and all Israel became paralyzed with fear.*

If you take your courage from another person, you will be left with nothing when that person is gone. If you trust in God, you will have the strength to go on even when circumstances collapse around you.

How do I find the courage to admit my mistakes?

2 SAMUEL 12:13 | *David confessed to Nathan, "I have sinned against the LORD." Nathan replied, "Yes, but the LORD has forgiven you, and you won't die for this sin."*

Admitting your mistakes and sins opens the door to forgiveness and restoration of relationships.

Promise from God   JOSHUA 1:9 | *This is my command—be strong and courageous! Do not be afraid or discouraged. For the* LORD *your God is with you wherever you go.*

CRITICISM

How do I offer criticism appropriately?

JOHN 8:7 | *Let the one who has never sinned throw the first stone!*

ROMANS 2:1 | *When you say they are wicked and should be punished, you are condemning yourself, for you who judge others do these very same things.*

Before criticizing another, take an inventory of your own sins and shortcomings so that you can approach the person with understanding and humility.

1 CORINTHIANS 13:5 | *[Love] does not demand its own way. It is not irritable, and it keeps no record of being wronged.*

Constructive criticism is always offered in love, with the motivation to build up. It addresses a specific need in someone else, not a list of his or her shortcomings or character flaws.

How should I respond to criticism? How do I evaluate whether criticism is constructive or destructive?

PROVERBS 12:16-18 | *A fool is quick-tempered, but a wise person stays calm when insulted. An honest witness tells the truth; a false witness tells lies. Some people make cutting remarks, but the words of the wise bring healing.*

ECCLESIASTES 7:5 | *Better to be criticized by a wise person than to be praised by a fool.*

Stay calm and don't lash back. Measure criticism according to the character of the person who is giving it—evaluate whether the criticism is coming from a person with a reputation for truth or for lies, and ask yourself whether the criticism is meant to heal or to hurt.

1 PETER 4:14 | *Be happy when you are insulted for being a Christian, for then the glorious Spirit of God rests upon you.*

Consider it a privilege to be criticized for your faith in God. God has special blessings for those who patiently endure this kind of criticism.

Promise from God 1 PETER 4:14 | *Be happy when you are insulted for being a Christian, for then the glorious Spirit of God rests upon you.*

CULTS

What is a cult?

JUDGES 2:19 | *The people returned to their corrupt ways. . . . They went after other gods, serving and worshiping them. And they refused to give up their evil practices and stubborn ways.*

A cult is a group of people who have their own religion and offer their wholehearted worship and devotion to anything or anyone other than God. Cults tend to be isolationist and very possessive, and they often involve bizarre rituals and follow a religious system instituted by a person with an engaging personality. Cults institute a religious system that is contrary to what God has established in the Bible.

How can I tell if an organization is a cult?

MATTHEW 7:15-17 | *Beware of false prophets who come disguised as harmless sheep but are really vicious wolves. You can identify them by their fruit, that is, by the way they act. Can you pick grapes from thornbushes, or figs from thistles? A good tree produces good fruit, and a bad tree produces bad fruit.*

You must compare the teachings of this group of people with the teachings in the Bible. That's why it is so important to know your Bible. If the teachings of a group of people are contrary to what is found in God's Word, and if these people tell you that their way is the only way to true peace and happiness, then you may be dealing with a cult. Another important way to judge a cult is to look at the behaviors of the members—do their lives honor God?

ROMANS 10:9 | *If you confess with your mouth that Jesus is Lord and believe in your heart that God raised him from the dead, you will be saved.*

Cults do not teach that faith in Jesus Christ as Savior alone, including forgiveness of sins through him alone, is the only way to heaven.

DANIEL 6:7 | *We are all in agreement—we administrators, officials, high officers, advisers, and governors—that the king should make a law that will be strictly enforced. Give orders that for the next thirty days any person who prays to anyone, divine or human—except to you, Your Majesty—will be thrown into the den of lions.*

There are many danger signs that can warn you that a group is a cult. Jesus said you can tell a person's heart by his or her actions (see Matthew 12:35). Although Daniel wasn't facing a cult, he was facing a group that was trying to divert his worship away from God. Cults will try to do the same thing.

Can God forgive me for having been in a cult?

ISAIAH 44:22 | *I have swept away your sins like a cloud. I have scattered your offenses like the morning mist. Oh, return to me, for I have paid the price to set you free.*

1 JOHN 1:9 | *If we confess our sins to him, he is faithful and just to forgive us our sins and to cleanse us from all wickedness.*

God longs for all people to turn to him. He forgives any and all of your sin if you sincerely ask him.

Promise from God 1 PETER 5:8-10 | *Stay alert! Watch out for your great enemy, the devil. He prowls around like a roaring lion, looking for someone to devour. Stand firm against him, and be strong in your faith. . . . God called you to share in his eternal glory by means of Christ Jesus.*

DATING

Is there a right or a wrong way to date? What kinds of boundaries should I set up in my dating relationships?

DEUTERONOMY 7:3-4 | *You must not intermarry. . . . Do not let your daughters and sons marry [ungodly people], for they will lead your children away from me to worship other gods.*

2 CORINTHIANS 6:14 | *Don't team up with those who are unbelievers. How can righteousness be a partner with wickedness? How can light live with darkness?*

The most important priority in the life of a Christian is your love for and obedience to God. But if the person you marry, the one with whom you will spend most of your life, does not believe in God, it will be difficult to keep God as your first priority. The Bible says that by marrying an unbeliever you set yourself up for being drawn away from God. While it is not necessarily wrong to date someone who is an unbeliever, you must be aware that steady dating with an unbeliever can lead to the kind of marriage God cautions against.

1 THESSALONIANS 4:3-5 | *God's will is for you to be holy, so stay away from all sexual sin. Then each of you will control his own body and live in holiness and honor—not in lustful passion like the pagans who do not know God and his ways.*

Guard against physical intimacy in a dating relationship. Such intimacy should be reserved only for marriage because it is a picture of the purity and devotion that you strive for in your relationship with God.

HEBREWS 13:18 | *Pray for us, for our conscience is clear and we want to live honorably in everything we do.*

It is essential to set boundaries and guidelines for your dating relationships before you get involved. These boundaries and guidelines should be based on the principles for relationships and marriage already created by God and found in the Bible. Boundaries should include issues such as appropriate physical touch, appropriate topics to discuss, treating each other with respect and honor, purity of speech, and building a spiritual basis to the relationship. When you go into a dating relationship committed to staying within your boundaries, you are building the foundation for a healthy relationship and you can end each date with a clear conscience.

PROVERBS 11:22 | *A beautiful woman who lacks discretion is like a gold ring in a pig's snout.*

PROVERBS 31:30 | *Charm is deceptive, and beauty does not last; but a woman who fears the LORD will be greatly praised.*

Good judgment is vital to making good decisions. This is especially true when deciding whom you will date. Beauty and lust have clouded people's judgment since the beginning of time.

How can I handle someone who is pushing me toward a physical relationship?

1 TIMOTHY 4:12 | *Don't let anyone think less of you because you are young. Be an example to all believers in what you say, in the way you live, in your love, your faith, and your purity.*

If you are dating someone who is pushing you to engage in activities you know are not in line with God's desire for relationships, don't allow your judgment to be dulled. Good judgment calls you to set up clear boundaries (which might cause an end to the relationship) so that you will not be led to compromise your relationship with God. It is better to stay pure than to give in to pressure. If the one you are dating is truly a friend who is caring and concerned about you, that person will honor and respect your desire for purity before marriage. If that person doesn't respect what is important to you before you are married, it is unlikely he or she will respect what is important to you after you are married.

Promise from God HEBREWS 13:4 | *Give honor to marriage, and remain faithful to one another in marriage. God will surely judge people who are immoral and those who commit adultery.*

DECEIT/DECEPTION

How can I know when I'm being deceived?

JUDGES 16:6 | *Delilah said to Samson, "Please tell me what makes you so strong and what it would take to tie you up securely."*

When your desire tells you yes and your conscience tells you no, can you still hear and follow your conscience? In this case, Samson let Delilah's beauty and promise of sexual pleasure convince him that she was sincere. Samson was a leader of Israel, yet he was spending the evening in the home of an ungodly woman who was sexually tempting him. What had happened to his conscience? When you make a practice of not listening to your conscience, soon you will hardly hear it.

ACTS 17:11 | *They searched the Scriptures day after day to see if Paul and Silas were teaching the truth.*

2 TIMOTHY 3:16 | *All Scripture is inspired by God and is useful to teach us what is true and to make us realize what is wrong in our lives. It corrects us when we are wrong and teaches us to do what is right.*

If someone is trying to convince you to do or believe something that contradicts Scripture, you can be assured it is wrong. Know the Bible well enough to discern when someone is telling you something false.

GENESIS 3:6 | *The woman was convinced. She saw that the tree was beautiful and its fruit looked delicious, and she wanted the wisdom it would give her. So she took some of the fruit and ate it.*

If something seems too good to be true, ask yourself if you are being deceived. Sometimes you are wildly blessed and it is for real. But most often, if something sounds too good to be true, it isn't.

PROVERBS 14:7 | *Stay away from fools, for you won't find knowledge on their lips.*

How often we ignore obvious truths! Stay away from deceitful and foolish people if you want to keep from being deceived.

How do I deceive myself?

JEREMIAH 17:9 | *The human heart is the most deceitful of all things.*

GALATIANS 6:7 | *Don't be misled—you cannot mock the justice of God. You will always harvest what you plant.*

You deceive yourself when you think you can get away with sin, and you deceive yourself when you think you can ignore God and still receive his blessings.

1 CORINTHIANS 3:18 | *Stop deceiving yourselves. If you think you are wise by this world's standards, you need to become a fool to be truly wise.*

You deceive yourself when you live as though this world is all there is. And you deceive yourself when you buy into the morals and values of your culture without evaluating them through the filter of God's Word.

Promise from God PSALM 32:2 | *What joy for those whose record the LORD has cleared of guilt, whose lives are lived in complete honesty!*

DECISIONS

What must I do to make good decisions?

PSALM 25:4 | *Show me the right path, O LORD; point out the road for me to follow.*

ROMANS 2:18 | *You know what [God] wants; you know what is right because you have been taught his law.*

Follow God's direction. God's Word shows you where God is going and gives you the wisdom to know how to follow where he leads.

LUKE 6:12-13 | *Jesus went up on a mountain to pray, and he prayed to God all night. At daybreak he called together all of his disciples and chose twelve of them to be apostles.*

Saturate your life with prayer. Prayer calms your spirit and clears your mind, making you more able to hear God's counsel.

PSALM 37:30 | *The godly offer good counsel; they teach right from wrong.*

PROVERBS 12:15 | *Fools think their own way is right, but the wise listen to others.*

Be open to good advice. Listen to advice of godly people and carefully consider it as you make a decision.

How does God guide my decision making?

PSALM 25:12 | *Who are those who fear the LORD? He will show them the path they should choose.*

PROVERBS 4:5 | *Get wisdom; develop good judgment. Don't forget my words or turn away from them.*

PHILIPPIANS 2:13 | *God is working in you, giving you the desire and the power to do what pleases him.*

Pray for God to give you the desire to obey him and seek his guidance. When you commit to obeying God's Word and God's will, he will guide you, and you will make decisions that please him and are therefore good for you.

How do I know if I've made a good decision?

2 TIMOTHY 3:16 | *All Scripture is inspired by God and is useful to teach us what is true and to make us realize what is wrong in our lives. It corrects us when we are wrong and teaches us to do what is right.*

You always make the right decision when you follow the commands God has given in the Bible. Also, always check your motives—are you deciding based on what you want or on what is best for others? Are you making a decision that is helping others or hurting them?

What is the most important decision I can make?

JOSHUA 24:15 | *Choose today whom you will serve. . . . As for me and my family, we will serve the LORD.*

JOHN 3:16 | *God loved the world so much that he gave his one and only Son, so that everyone who believes in him will not perish but have eternal life.*

The most important decision you, or anyone else, will make is whether or not you will be a follower of the one true God. This decision requires believing that his Son, Jesus, died for your sins and rose from the dead so that you can have a relationship with God forever. This is a decision that has eternal implications.

Promise from God PROVERBS 3:6 | *Seek [the Lord's] will in all you do, and he will show you which path to take.*

DEPRESSION

What causes depression? How am I vulnerable to it?

1 KINGS 19:3-4 | *Elijah was afraid and fled for his life. He went to Beersheba, a town in Judah, and he left his servant there. Then he went on alone into the wilderness, traveling all day. He sat down under a solitary broom tree and prayed that he might die. "I have had enough, LORD," he said. "Take my life, for I am no better than my ancestors who have already died."*

You are especially vulnerable to depression after a major victory. Elijah had just defeated 450 prophets of Baal and saw God work several mighty miracles (see 1 Kings 17–18), yet he was afraid and depressed. Between his exhaustion and his emotions spiraling downward after the high of victory, he was susceptible to depression.

PROVERBS 13:12 | *Hope deferred makes the heart sick, but a dream fulfilled is a tree of life.*

A heart without hope is a heart ripe for depression.

ROMANS 7:21-24 | *When I want to do what is right, I inevitably do what is wrong. I love God's law with all my heart. But there is another power within me that is at war with my mind. This power makes me a slave to the sin that is still within me. Oh, what a miserable person I am! Who will free me from this life that is dominated by sin and death?*

Depression can occur when you realize how wide the gap is between the ideal you strive for and the reality you see within and around you. This can create a great sense of failure.

PSALM 42:3-5 | *Day and night I have only tears for food, while my enemies continually taunt me, saying, "Where is this God of yours?" My heart is breaking as I remember how it used to be: I walked among the crowds of worshipers, leading a great procession to the house of God, singing for joy and giving thanks amid the sound of a great celebration! Why am I discouraged? Why is my heart so sad?*

Depression often comes from looking into the past at what you have lost.

1 SAMUEL 16:14 | *The Spirit of the LORD had left Saul, and the LORD sent a tormenting spirit that filled him with depression and fear.*

When you neglect the Lord to the point where he can no longer get your attention, he may leave you alone for a while, and depression can move easily into the vacant room in your heart. The further you move from God, the less hope you have of receiving the joy of his blessings.

ECCLESIASTES 4:8 | *[An example of something meaningless] is the case of a man who is all alone, without a child or a brother, yet who works hard to gain as much wealth as he can. But then he asks himself, "Who am I working for? Why am I giving up so much pleasure now?" It is all so meaningless and depressing.*

If you spend your life pursuing meaningless things, you may become depressed when you recognize that what you have done has little lasting value.

Does God care when I feel depressed?

PSALM 34:18 | *The LORD is close to the brokenhearted; he rescues those whose spirits are crushed.*

MATTHEW 5:4 | *God blesses those who mourn, for they will be comforted.*

God isn't disappointed by your depression and emotional struggles; on the contrary, he feels a special closeness to you. You can actually experience more of God's presence in times of brokenness.

PSALM 139:12 | *Even in darkness I cannot hide from you.*

There is no depth to which you can descend where God is not present with you. Even if you don't feel his presence, he has not abandoned you. You don't have to feel trapped in the darkness if you allow God's comforting light to enter your soul.

PSALM 130:1 | *From the depths of despair, O LORD, I call for your help.*

Allow yourself to cry out to God from even the darkest pit of despair. He wants to help you.

ISAIAH 53:3 | *He was despised and rejected—a man of sorrows, acquainted with deepest grief.*

Remember that Jesus understands the pain of human life, and he suffered everything you have and more.

ROMANS 8:39 | *No power in the sky above or in the earth below—indeed, nothing in all creation will ever be able to separate us from the love of God that is revealed in Christ Jesus our Lord.*

Not even life's worst depression can separate you from the love Jesus has for you and wants to lavish on you. He knows all that has happened and what you are going through, and he loves you with a greater love than you could ever imagine.

Can any good come out of my depression?

PSALM 126:5 | *Those who plant in tears will harvest with shouts of joy.*

2 CORINTHIANS 12:9 | *[God] said, "My grace is all you need. My power works best in weakness." So now I am glad to boast about my weaknesses, so that the power of Christ can work through me.*

When you are weak, you are more receptive to the Lord's strength. When everything is going your way, it's easy to overlook God's hand in your life. As God works through your weakness, however, you learn to depend more on him and recognize and be grateful for the good work that he can accomplish in you.

How can I help others who are struggling with depression?

PROVERBS 25:20 | *Singing cheerful songs to a person with a heavy heart is like taking someone's coat in cold weather or pouring vinegar in a wound.*

ROMANS 12:15 | *Be happy with those who are happy, and weep with those who weep.*

2 CORINTHIANS 1:4 | *He comforts us in all our troubles so that we can comfort others. When they are troubled, we will be able to give them the same comfort God has given us.*

You can help people who are depressed by your quiet presence, your love, and your encouragement. Telling them to "snap out of it" or minimizing their pain by false cheeriness will just make them feel worse. The best way to help those who are down is to model the gentle, caring love of Christ.

Promise from God MATTHEW 11:28 | *Jesus said, "Come to me, all of you who are weary and carry heavy burdens, and I will give you rest."*

DESIRES

Is it okay to want something?

1 KINGS 3:5 | *The LORD appeared to Solomon in a dream, and God said, "What do you want? Ask, and I will give it to you!"*

PROVERBS 13:12 | *Hope deferred makes the heart sick, but a dream fulfilled is a tree of life.*

God created desire within you as a means of expressing yourself. Desire is good and healthy if directed toward the proper object: that which is good and right and God-honoring. It is ironic that a desire can be right or wrong, depending on your motive and the object of your desire. For example, the desire to love someone of the opposite sex, if directed to your spouse, is healthy and right. But that same desire directed to someone who is not your spouse is adultery. The desire to lead an organization is healthy if your motive is to serve others, but unhealthy and wrong if your motive is the power to control others.

PSALM 73:25 | *I desire [God] more than anything on earth.*

ISAIAH 26:8 | *LORD, we show our trust in you by obeying your laws; our heart's desire is to glorify your name.*

Your greatest desire must be a relationship with God because that will influence all your other desires.

PHILIPPIANS 4:8 | *Fix your thoughts on what is true, and honorable, and right, and pure, and lovely, and admirable. Think about things that are excellent and worthy of praise.*

Desiring sin is always wrong. What you think about often leads to the actions you take. Therefore, focusing your thoughts on what is good creates healthy desires and leads to good actions.

How do I resist wrong desires?

JAMES 3:13 | *If you are wise and understand God's ways, prove it by living an honorable life, doing good works with the humility that comes from wisdom.*

Keep yourself busy with good deeds.

MATTHEW 6:13 | *Don't let us yield to temptation, but rescue us from the evil one.*

Pray for strength to overcome temptation, that good desires will overcome bad ones.

2 CHRONICLES 34:33 | *Josiah removed all detestable idols from the entire land.*

Take away the sources of temptation.

COLOSSIANS 3:2 | *Think about the things of heaven, not the things of earth.*

Fill your mind with God and thoughts that honor him.

PROVERBS 15:22 | *Plans go wrong for lack of advice; many advisers bring success.*

Find a person willing to help you. You (and everyone else) need someone who will encourage you and hold you accountable.

Can God help me change the desires within my heart? How?

ROMANS 7:6 | *We can serve God, not in the old way . . . but in the new way of living in the Spirit.*

When you give control of your life to God, he gives you a new heart, a new nature, and a new desire to please him.

EZRA 1:5 | *God stirred the hearts of the priests and Levites . . . to go to Jerusalem to rebuild the Temple of the LORD.*

God stirs your heart with right desires. It is up to you to ask him for help to act upon them.

Promise from God EZEKIEL 36:26 | *I will give you a new heart, and I will put a new spirit in you. I will take out your stony, stubborn heart and give you a tender, responsive heart.*

DISTRACTIONS

What is the danger in distractions?

MATTHEW 14:28-31 | *Peter called to him, "Lord, if it's really you, tell me to come to you, walking on the water." "Yes, come," Jesus said. So Peter went over the side of the boat and walked on the water toward Jesus. But when he saw the strong wind and the waves, he was terrified and began to sink. "Save me, Lord!" he shouted. Jesus immediately reached out and grabbed him. "You have so little faith," Jesus said. "Why did you doubt me?"*

LUKE 9:62 | *Jesus [said], "Anyone who puts a hand to the plow and then looks back is not fit for the Kingdom of God."*

Distractions can take your focus off Jesus. You can be in the middle of doing great things, but if you take your eyes off Jesus for even a moment, you can begin to sink!

How can God use distractions?

MATTHEW 19:13-15 | *One day some parents brought their children to Jesus so he could lay his hands on them and pray for them. But the disciples scolded the parents for bothering him. But Jesus said, "Let the children come to me. Don't stop them! For the Kingdom of Heaven belongs to those who are like these children." And he placed his hands on their heads and blessed them before he left.*

MARK 10:17 | *As Jesus was starting out on his way to Jerusalem, a man came running up to him, knelt down, and asked, "Good Teacher, what must I do to inherit eternal life?"*

Distractions bombarded Jesus all the time. But he didn't see them all as distractions; he saw some as opportunities to save the lost or to help someone. When someone needs you, what would otherwise be a distraction can become a divine opportunity to show the love and care of God. Don't miss the chance to focus on the people God brings to you for help.

ACTS 16:29-32 | *The jailer called for lights and ran to the dungeon and fell down trembling before Paul and Silas. Then he brought them out and asked, "Sirs, what must I do to be saved?" They replied, "Believe in the Lord Jesus and you will be saved, along with everyone in your household." And they shared the word of the Lord with him and with all who lived in his household.*

Most people would look at a jail sentence as a definite distraction to their ability to serve God. Not Paul and Silas! Their location didn't deter them from their mission. Maybe God wants you to focus for a while on what or who is right in front of you. Your "distraction" may be a calling from God to minister to new people in a new place.

How do I remain focused amid distractions?

HEBREWS 12:13 | *Mark out a straight path for your feet so that those who are weak and lame will not fall but become strong.*

Make clear goals for how you will live your Christian life, and then follow those goals without wavering.

ACTS 6:3-4 | *Select seven men who are well respected and are full of the Spirit and wisdom. We will give them this responsibility [of the daily food distribution]. Then we apostles can spend our time in prayer and teaching the word.*

Stay focused on what you do well, and learn to delegate to others tasks they can do as well as or better than you.

PSALM 119:157 | *Many persecute and trouble me, yet I have not swerved from your laws.*

DANIEL 6:13 | *[The officials] told the king, "That man Daniel, one of the captives from Judah, is ignoring you and your law. He still prays to his God three times a day."*

Don't let anything distract you from what you know you should be doing or what you know is right.

PHILIPPIANS 3:13 | *I focus on this one thing: Forgetting the past and looking forward to what lies ahead.*

Don't let your past drag you down; that can be very distracting. Focus your energies on what you can do for God and others now and in the future.

PSALM 66:9 | *Our lives are in his hands, and he keeps our feet from stumbling.*

Keep your eyes fixed on the Lord. If you don't constantly stay focused on God, you are letting down your guard and making it easier for the world to distract your heart and mind.

Promise from God HEBREWS 12:13 | *Mark out a straight path for your feet so that those who are weak and lame will not fall but become strong.*

DOUBT

Is it a sin to doubt God? Does it mean I am lacking faith?

MATTHEW 11:2-3 | *John the Baptist . . . sent his disciples to ask Jesus, "Are you the Messiah we've been expecting, or should we keep looking for someone else?"*

2 PETER 1:4-5 | *He has given us great and precious promises . . . [so] make every effort to respond to God's promises.*

Many people in the Bible whom we consider to be "pillars of faith" had moments of doubt. This doesn't mean that they had less faith but that their faith was being challenged in a new way. Allow your doubt to move you closer to God, not further away from him. As you move closer to him, you will find the strength to trust him and your faith will grow even stronger.

PSALM 94:19 | *When doubts filled my mind, your comfort gave me renewed hope and cheer.*

MATTHEW 14:31 | *Jesus immediately reached out and grabbed him. "You have so little faith," Jesus said. "Why did you doubt me?"*

David, John the Baptist, and Peter, along with many other biblical heroes, struggled with various doubts about God and his ability or desire to help. God doesn't mind doubt as long as you are seeking answers from him in the midst of it. Doubt can become sin if it leads you away from God to skepticism, to cynicism, then to hard-heartedness.

GENESIS 3:2-4 | *"We may eat fruit from the trees in the garden,"
the woman replied. "It's only the fruit from the tree in the
middle of the garden that we are not allowed to eat. God said,
'You must not eat it or even touch it; if you do, you will die.'"
"You won't die!" the serpent replied to the woman.*

One of Satan's tactics is to get you to doubt God's goodness. He tries to get you to forget all God has given you and
to focus on what you don't have. If you are spending much
of your time thinking about what you don't have, you may
be slipping into unhealthy doubt.

PSALM 95:9 | *[The Lord said,] "Your ancestors tested and tried
my patience, even though they saw everything I did."*

God gives everyone plenty of evidence to believe in him.
Doubt comes when you fail to stop long enough to observe
all the evidence. And when doubt turns to disbelief, you are
in danger of ignoring God altogether.

What should I do when I find myself doubting God?

MARK 9:24 | *The father instantly cried out, "I do believe, but
help me overcome my unbelief!"*

Bring your doubts directly to God in prayer. Be candid and
honest as you pour out your heart to the Lord. Pray that
God will give you the strong faith you need.

MARK 8:17-19 | *Jesus . . . said, "Why are you [so worried] about
having no bread? . . . Don't you remember anything at all?
When I fed the 5,000 with five loaves of bread, how many
baskets of leftovers did you pick up afterward?"*

When you are struggling with doubt, take time to remember the way God has worked in your life. As you recall God's "track record," you will grow confident that he will work in your present situation as well.

JOHN 20:27 | *[Jesus] said to Thomas, "Put your finger here, and look at my hands. Put your hand into the wound in my side. Don't be faithless any longer. Believe!"*

When you have doubts, review the evidence. There is a great deal of historical evidence to verify the accuracy of the Bible's claims.

HABAKKUK 2:1 | *I will wait to see what the LORD says and how he will answer my complaint.*

Be patient. Let God answer your questions on his schedule, not yours. Don't throw away your faith just because God doesn't resolve your doubt immediately.

1 THESSALONIANS 5:11 | *Encourage each other and build each other up, just as you are already doing.*

HEBREWS 10:25 | *Let us not neglect our meeting together.*

When you are wrestling with doubt, keep attending church and stay close to other Christians. Resist the temptation to isolate yourself, for that will serve only to weaken your faith more. Doubt feeds on loneliness.

Are there things I should never doubt?

JOHN 6:37 | *[Jesus said,] "Those the Father has given me will come to me, and I will never reject them."*

JOHN 10:28-29 | *[Jesus said,] "I give them eternal life, and they will never perish. No one can snatch them away from me, for my Father has given them to me, and he is more powerful than anyone else. No one can snatch them from the Father's hand."*

EPHESIANS 1:14 | *The Spirit is God's guarantee that he will give us the inheritance he promised and that he has purchased us to be his own people.*

Never doubt your salvation. Once you have become a Christian, Satan can never snatch you away from God.

Promise from God HEBREWS 13:5 | *God has said, "I will never fail you. I will never abandon you."*

DRINKING

When does drinking become wrong?

EXODUS 32:6 | *The people got up early the next morning to sacrifice burnt offerings and peace offerings. After this, they celebrated with feasting and drinking, and they indulged in pagan revelry.*

EPHESIANS 5:18 | *Don't be drunk with wine, because that will ruin your life. Instead, be filled with the Holy Spirit.*

Drinking becomes wrong when it leads to drunkenness, when it influences your thoughts or actions, or when it causes you to disobey and dishonor God. (For minors, this includes drinking at any time.)

I'm addicted to alcohol. Can God help me?

2 CORINTHIANS 5:17 | *Anyone who belongs to Christ has become a new person. The old life is gone; a new life has begun!*

God can and will help anyone who is trapped by an addiction if that person will confess the sin, call upon him for help, and follow the path back to healthy living. God helps by showing you how to rely on the power of the Holy Spirit, by showing you the principles of self-control found in his Word, and by giving you the wisdom of counselors and other believers who can help you learn how to combat your addiction.

Promise from God 1 CORINTHIANS 10:13 | *The temptations in your life are no different from what others experience. And God is faithful. He will not allow the temptation to be more than you can stand. When you are tempted, he will show you a way out so that you can endure.*

DRUGS

What does the Bible say about drugs?

1 CORINTHIANS 6:12-13 | *You say, "I am allowed to do anything"— but not everything is good for you. And even though "I am allowed to do anything," I must not become a slave to anything. . . . Our bodies . . . were made for the Lord, and the Lord cares about our bodies.*

1 CORINTHIANS 6:19-20 | *Don't you realize that your body is the temple of the Holy Spirit, who lives in you and was given to you by God? You do not belong to yourself, for God bought you with a high price. So you must honor God with your body.*

1 CORINTHIANS 10:31 | *Whether you eat or drink, or whatever you do, do it all for the glory of God.*

The Bible doesn't specifically mention the kind of drug addictions common today, but it does address the ever-present problem of putting things into your body that are harmful to it and that impair your ability to function well. Taking drugs to get a "high" is an artificial feeling of happiness, a cheap substitute for the true joy that comes when you are filled with and controlled by the Holy Spirit. When the Holy Spirit controls your life, your joy is authentic and contagious.

Some say that everything in moderation is okay. Can't that apply to drugs, too?

2 PETER 2:19 | *[False teachers] promise freedom, but they themselves are slaves of sin and corruption. For you are a slave to whatever controls you.*

Whatever has control over you is your master. If God is your master, he will raise you up and encourage you, but drugs will only tear you down and make you a slave to their addictive power. Some things are not good for you, even in moderation. Even a little sin is deadly.

Promise from God ROMANS 8:5 | *Those who are dominated by the sinful nature think about sinful things, but those who are controlled by the Holy Spirit think about things that please the Spirit.*

ENEMIES

What does it mean to love my enemies?

MATTHEW 18:21-22 | *Peter . . . asked, "Lord, how often should I forgive someone who sins against me? Seven times?" "No, not seven times," Jesus replied, "but seventy times seven!"*

Respond to your enemies—no matter what they try to do—with forgiveness.

MATTHEW 5:43-44 | *[Jesus said,] "You have heard the law that says, 'Love your neighbor' and hate your enemy. But I say, love your enemies! Pray for those who persecute you!"*

ROMANS 12:20-21 | *If your enemies are hungry, feed them. If they are thirsty, give them something to drink. In doing this, you will heap burning coals of shame on their heads. Don't let evil conquer you, but conquer evil by doing good.*

Loving your enemies seems unreasonable—until you realize that you were an enemy of God until he forgave you. When you love an enemy, you see him or her as Christ does—a person in need of grace. Getting to that point takes prayer. You can't pray for someone and not feel compassion for that person.

Is it possible to turn an enemy into a friend?

ACTS 9:1-6 | *Saul was uttering threats with every breath and was eager to kill the Lord's followers. . . . He wanted to bring them—both men and women—back to Jerusalem in chains. As he was approaching Damascus on this mission, a light from heaven suddenly shone down around him. He fell to the ground and heard a voice saying to him, "Saul! Saul! Why are you persecuting me?" "Who are you, lord?" Saul asked. And the voice replied, "I am Jesus, the one you are persecuting! Now get up and go into the city, and you will be told what you must do."*

GALATIANS 1:23 | *People were saying, "The one who used to persecute us is now preaching the very faith he tried to destroy!"*

Every day enemies of God become believers in God! It is a mystery why he overwhelms some enemies, such as Saul (whose name was changed to Paul), so that they turn to his side and why he seems to leave other enemies alone, at least in this world. But in almost every church around the world there are believers who once actively opposed God, God's people, and God's way of living.

Are there really spiritual enemies—powers of darkness—trying to attack me?

DANIEL 10:12-13 | *[The man in the vision] said, "Don't be afraid, Daniel. Since the first day you began to pray for understanding and to humble yourself before your God, your request has been heard in heaven. I have come in answer to your prayer. But for twenty-one days the spirit prince of the kingdom of Persia blocked my way. Then Michael, one of the archangels, came to help me."*

MATTHEW 4:1 | *Jesus was led by the Spirit into the wilderness to be tempted there by the devil.*

The Bible clearly teaches that human beings are involved in a spiritual battle with the forces of evil. Far from excluding you from this spiritual battle, faith puts you right in the middle of it. You are in a battle for your very soul. You must recognize that and arm yourself or you will be defeated.

EPHESIANS 6:12 | *We are not fighting against flesh-and-blood enemies, but against evil rulers and authorities of the unseen world, against mighty powers in this dark world, and against evil spirits in the heavenly places.*

The purpose of Satan and his cohorts is to defy God and wear down believers until they are led into sin. This gives the evil one pleasure and greater opportunity. But God is a warrior. A battle rages in the spiritual realm, and as a believer, you are right in the thick of it. God is always ready to fight on your behalf, always ready to come to your defense. In addition, he provides you with armor so that you can fight alongside him (see Ephesians 6:11-18). But you must join God in the battle or you will be vulnerable and helpless to withstand the enemy. If you join, you are guaranteed victory.

Promise from God 2 THESSALONIANS 3:3 | *The Lord is faithful; he will strengthen you and guard you from the evil one.*

ENVIRONMENT

What does the Bible say about the environment and my responsibility in environmental issues?

GENESIS 1:28 | *God blessed [the man and the woman he had made] and said, "Be fruitful and multiply. Fill the earth and govern it. Reign over . . . all the animals."*

Human beings were created to share responsibility for the earth by being good stewards of the created environment.

GENESIS 2:15 | *The LORD God placed the man in the Garden of Eden to tend and watch over it.*

The first assignment God gave to Adam was to tend and care for the Garden of Eden, and God expects you to care for your little corner of the world as well.

DEUTERONOMY 20:19-20 | *When you are attacking a town and the war drags on, you must not cut down the trees. . . . Are the trees your enemies, that you should attack them?*

Even in time of war, God is concerned about the needless destruction of the environment.

LEVITICUS 25:4 | *During the seventh year the land must have . . . a year of complete rest.*

God instructed the people of Israel to let their farmland rest every seventh year for the conservation of good, productive soil.

PSALM 96:11-13 | *Let the heavens be glad, and the earth rejoice! Let the sea and everything in it shout his praise! Let the fields and their crops burst out with joy! Let the trees of the forest rustle with praise before the LORD, for he is coming!*

God created nature to proclaim his glory. You should do all you can to preserve this testimony for God.

Promise from God PSALM 19:1-4 | *The heavens proclaim the glory of God. The skies display his craftsmanship. Day after day they continue to speak; night after night they make him known. They speak without a sound or word; their voice is never heard. Yet their message has gone throughout the earth, and their words to all the world.*

EVIL

Why do people often seem to get away with evil?

JEREMIAH 12:1-2 | *Why are the wicked so prosperous? Why are evil people so happy? You have planted them, and they have taken root and prospered. Your name is on their lips, but you are far from their hearts.*

Even Jeremiah struggled with the prosperity of evil people. You must remember that because of sin, life on this earth is not fair. But at the final judgment, God will settle all accounts, and everything will be fair for all eternity.

ISAIAH 32:7-8 | *The smooth tricks of scoundrels are evil. They plot crooked schemes. They lie to convict the poor, even when the cause of the poor is just. But generous people plan to do what is generous, and they stand firm in their generosity.*

It seems that people today can do anything they want and not only get away with it but also flourish. However, God has promised that in his time everyone will be judged, evil will be exposed, and the righteous will prevail. God doesn't promise the absence of evil on this earth. In fact, he warns that evil will be pervasive and powerful. But God promises to help you stand against evil; if you do, you will receive your reward in heaven, where evil will be no more.

How can I combat evil?

1 JOHN 4:4 | *The Spirit who lives in you is greater than the spirit who lives in the world.*

1 JOHN 5:4 | *Every child of God defeats this evil world, and we achieve this victory through our faith.*

Your first line of defense is to draw strength from the fact that God is more powerful than your problems and your enemy, the evil one.

ROMANS 13:14 | *Clothe yourself with the presence of the Lord Jesus Christ. And don't let yourself think about ways to indulge your evil desires.*

Surrender yourself to Christ's control. Make sure that you don't put yourself in situations where you know your resolve to be righteous will be tested. The closer you walk with Christ, the easier it is to avoid the snare of evil.

ROMANS 12:21 | *Don't let evil conquer you, but conquer evil by doing good.*

Combat evil with goodness. This is a difficult thing to do, but ultimately it is the only thing that will work, for righteousness is stronger than evil.

Promise from God   1 JOHN 5:4 | *Every child of God defeats this evil world, and we achieve this victory through our faith.*

EVOLUTION

If things did not evolve, how were the earth and life formed?

GENESIS 1:1 | *In the beginning God created the heavens and the earth.*

GENESIS 1:27 | *God created human beings in his own image. In the image of God he created them; male and female he created them.*

Interestingly, the discoveries of modern astrophysicists have confirmed that the universe had a finite beginning. If the universe had a beginning, it stands to reason there must have been a creator. Something cannot come from nothing. The Bible teaches that God is eternal—that is, he exists outside of space and time—and therefore is the "beginner" of all things. He chose to create the universe and its inhabitants as an expression of his love. God not only began life but continues to express his love to his creation through the gift of his Son, Jesus Christ, in order to have a personal love relationship with mankind (see John 3:16). Science has clearly shown us that virtually all life forms evolve in some manner over time, adapting to their environment. This is not contrary to anything in the Bible. What is contrary to the Bible is the assumption by some that human beings evolved from some primitive life form. Human beings are unique in that they have within them the very breath of God, which also gives them a morality and a consciousness that no other life forms have.

GENESIS 1:25-26 | *God made all sorts of wild animals, livestock, and small animals, each able to produce offspring of the same kind. And God saw that it was good. Then God said, "Let us make human beings in our image, to be like us. They will reign over the fish in the sea, the birds in the sky, the livestock, all the wild animals on the earth, and the small animals that scurry along the ground."*

ROMANS 11:36 | *Everything comes from him and exists by his power and is intended for his glory.*

The Bible clearly states that God made the heavens, the earth, and all that inhabits them. It takes more faith to believe that this vast, complex world evolved from some primordial soup than to believe it was called into existence by the divine Creator.

Promise from God ISAIAH 43:13 | *From eternity to eternity I am God. . . . No one can undo what I have done.*

EXCUSES

What are the first excuses in the Bible?

GENESIS 3:11-12 | *[The Lord God asked,] "Have you eaten from the tree whose fruit I commanded you not to eat?" The man replied, "It was the woman you gave me who gave me the fruit, and I ate it."*

Adam made the first excuse. He blamed Eve, and indirectly he blamed God because God had given him "the woman." Then Eve blamed the serpent (see Genesis 3:13). Both tried to excuse their actions by blaming someone else.

What are some examples of other people who had poor excuses?

GENESIS 16:5 | *Sarai said to Abram, "This is all your fault! I put my servant into your arms, but now that she's pregnant she treats me with contempt."*

Sarai, Abram's wife, couldn't have children, so she gave her slave to Abram in order to have a child through her. Later Sarai had second thoughts and blamed Abram for so easily accepting her offer.

EXODUS 32:24 | *[Aaron said to Moses,] "I told [the people], 'Whoever has gold jewelry, take it off.' When they brought it to me, I simply threw it into the fire—and out came this calf!"*

Aaron's lame excuse for making an idol—something expressly condemned by God—was that it just happened! It is easy to do the same thing, blaming your sin on circumstances beyond your control. But you are completely accountable for all your actions (see Romans 14:12; Revelation 20:12).

1 SAMUEL 15:1, 3, 9, 15 | *Samuel said to Saul, . . . "Listen to this message from the LORD! . . . Go and completely destroy the entire Amalekite nation." . . . [But] Saul and his men . . . kept the best. . . . "It's true that the army spared the best of the sheep, goats, and cattle," Saul admitted [to Samuel]. "But they are going to sacrifice them to the LORD your God. We have destroyed everything else."*

Saul tried to justify his sinful actions with the excuse that he sinned in order to do a good thing. His life was a story of one excuse after another. Finally, he ran out of excuses and lost his kingdom (see 1 Samuel 15:26) because he simply wouldn't own up to his mistakes and admit that he was wrong.

LUKE 22:57 | *[Peter said,] "Woman, . . . I don't even know him."*

Peter had an excuse for pretending that he did not know Jesus—he wanted to save his life or at least avoid the ridicule of being associated with Jesus. Ironically, it is when you start making excuses about knowing Jesus that you are in the greatest danger of losing all that he offers.

Can I ever excuse myself from God's work because I lack abilities or resources?

EXODUS 4:10 | *Moses pleaded with the LORD, "O Lord, I'm not very good with words."*

JUDGES 6:15-16 | *"But Lord," Gideon replied, "how can I rescue Israel? My clan is the weakest in the whole tribe of Manasseh, and I am the least in my entire family!" The LORD said to him, "I will be with you."*

Both Moses and Gideon thought they had a good excuse for not serving God. But the qualifications God looks for are different from what you might expect. He often chooses the least likely people to do his work in order to more effectively demonstrate his power (see 1 Corinthians 1:20-28). If you know that God has called you to do something, stop trying to excuse yourself. He will give you the help and strength you need to get the job done.

Can I be excused for not accepting the Lord?

PHILIPPIANS 2:10-11 | *At the name of Jesus every knee should bow, in heaven and on earth and under the earth, and every tongue confess that Jesus Christ is Lord, to the glory of God the Father.*

You may have all kinds of excuses for avoiding God—being too busy, blaming God for your hardships, procrastinating, not wanting to give up your favorite vices, or even not knowing where to begin. Do you think any of those excuses will hold up when you see God face-to-face?

ROMANS 1:20 | *Ever since the world was created, people have seen the earth and sky. Through everything God made, they can clearly see his invisible qualities—his eternal power and divine nature. So they have no excuse for not knowing God.*

Everyone has seen the testimony of nature, God's work, which the Bible says clearly reveals the hand of an almighty Creator. That alone witnesses to his presence and power. If you fail to come to terms with God, you really are without excuse.

Promise from God 1 PETER 1:17 | *Remember that the heavenly Father to whom you pray has no favorites. He will judge or reward you according to what you do.*

FAILURE

What must I learn about failure?

GENESIS 3:12-13 | *[Adam said to God], "It was the woman you gave me who gave me the fruit, and I ate it." . . . "The serpent deceived me," [Eve] replied.*

2 CORINTHIANS 12:9 | *[God] said, "My grace is all you need. My power works best in weakness."*

One thing is certain: You must learn to live with failure. Everyone has weaknesses. The key to character is not how seldom you fail, but how you respond to failure. Adam and Eve, for example, responded to their failures by trying to blame each other rather than admitting their mistakes and seeking forgiveness.

JONAH 1:3 | *Jonah . . . went in the opposite direction to get away from the LORD.*

Don't make the mistake of running from God. That is the worst kind of failure and will bring the worst kind of consequences.

COLOSSIANS 3:23-24 | *Work willingly at whatever you do, as though you were working for the Lord rather than for people. Remember that the Lord will give you an inheritance as your reward, and that the Master you are serving is Christ.*

Your sense of failure may have been wrongfully determined by the lack of approval of others. Scripture reminds you to define success in terms of faithfulness to God. God will reward your faithfulness even if you fail in the eyes of the world.

GENESIS 4:6-7 | *"Why are you so angry?" the LORD asked Cain. "Why do you look so dejected? You will be accepted if you do what is right. But if you refuse to do what is right, then watch out! Sin is crouching at the door, eager to control you. But you must subdue it and be its master."*

PROVERBS 29:1 | *Whoever stubbornly refuses to accept criticism will suddenly be destroyed beyond recovery.*

If you are told you have made a mistake, you must look at the source and the substance of the criticism, then reflect and learn for the future.

JUDGES 16:17, 21, 28 | *Finally, Samson shared his secret with her. . . . So the Philistines captured him and gouged out his eyes. . . . Then Samson prayed to the LORD, "Sovereign LORD, remember me again."*

God can still use you despite your failure. Samson's life, though filled with great failures, was still used mightily by God.

When I have failed, how do I get past the failure and go on?

1 KINGS 8:23, 33-34 | *[Solomon] prayed, "O LORD . . . if your people Israel are defeated by their enemies because they have sinned against you, and if they turn to you and acknowledge your name and pray to you . . . , then hear from heaven and forgive the sin of your people."*

If your failure is the result of something you did wrong, turning to God and admitting your sin to him is the first and best response you can make.

MICAH 7:8 | *Though I fall, I will rise again. Though I sit in darkness, the LORD will be my light.*

When you fail, you must get up again. Many of life's inspiring success stories come from people who failed many times but never gave up. Most important, never give up on your relationship with God, who promises you the ultimate victory of eternal life.

Promise from God PSALM 37:23-24 | *The LORD directs the steps of the godly. He delights in every detail of their lives. Though they stumble, they will never fall, for the LORD holds them by the hand.*

FAITH

Why should I have faith in God?

JOHN 3:16 | *God loved the world so much that he gave his one and only Son, so that everyone who believes in him will not perish but have eternal life.*

JOHN 5:24 | *[Jesus said,] "I tell you the truth, those who listen to my message and believe in God who sent me have eternal life."*

According to the Bible (God's own words), faith in God means believing that he sent his Son, Jesus Christ, to earth to save you from eternal death and provide you an eternal home in heaven. The One who created heaven has told you clearly how to get there: Believing that Jesus died for your sins and rose again from the dead is the only way to receive this gift of eternal life.

HEBREWS 11:1 | *Faith is the confidence that what we hope for will actually happen; it gives us assurance about things we cannot see.*

Faith gives you hope. When the world seems to be a crazy, mixed-up place, you can be absolutely confident that one day Jesus will come and make it right again. Your faith in his promise to do that some day will allow you to keep going today.

Faith seems so complicated; how do I go about getting it?

MARK 5:36 | *Jesus . . . said to Jairus, "Don't be afraid. Just have faith."*

Too often we make faith too complicated. It simply means trusting Jesus to do what he has promised—and he promised to give you life forever in heaven if you just believe he is who he said he is, the Son of God.

How much faith must I have?

MATTHEW 17:20 | *[Jesus said,] "I tell you the truth, if you had faith even as small as a mustard seed, you could say to this mountain, 'Move from here to there,' and it would move. Nothing would be impossible."*

The mustard seed was often used to illustrate the smallest seed known to people. Jesus said it is not the size of your faith but the size of the One in whom you believe that makes the difference. You do not have to have great faith in God; rather you have to have faith in a great God.

How can I strengthen my faith?

GENESIS 12:1, 4 | *The LORD had said to Abram, "Leave your native country . . . and go to the land that I will show you." . . . So Abram departed as the LORD had instructed.*

Like a muscle, faith gets stronger the more you exercise it. When you do what God asks you to do and then see him bless you as a result of your obedience, your faith grows.

PSALM 119:48 | *I honor and love your commands. I meditate on your decrees.*

ROMANS 10:17 | *Faith comes from hearing . . . the Good News about Christ.*

Faith is grounded in God's Word. Your faith will grow stronger as you study the Bible and reflect on the truths about who God is, his guidelines for your life, and how he wants to do his work on earth through you.

2 KINGS 6:17 | *Elisha prayed, "O LORD, open his eyes and let him see!" The LORD opened the young man's eyes, and when he looked up, he saw that the hillside around Elisha was filled with horses and chariots of fire.*

JOHN 20:27-29 | *[Jesus] said to Thomas, "Put your finger here, and look at my hands. Put your hand into the wound in my side. Don't be faithless any longer. Believe!" "My Lord and my God!" Thomas exclaimed. Then Jesus told him, "You believe because you have seen me. Blessed are those who believe without seeing me."*

The strongest faith is not one based on physical senses but on spiritual conviction. There is a spiritual element to this world that you cannot see, but it is very real. Your faith will become stronger the more you allow the Holy Spirit to strengthen your "spiritual vision"; then you will sense and see the results of God working in your life and in the lives of those around you.

How does faith in God impact my life?

GENESIS 15:6 | *Abram believed the LORD, and the LORD counted him as righteous because of his faith.*

COLOSSIANS 1:22 | *[God] has reconciled you to himself through the death of Christ in his physical body. As a result, he has brought you into his own presence, and you are holy and blameless as you stand before him without a single fault.*

Faith is your lifeline to God. Sin breaks your relationship with God—cutting your lifeline to him. A holy God cannot live with unholy people. But the simple act of faith when you accept Jesus as Savior and ask him to forgive your sins makes you righteous in God's sight.

ISAIAH 26:3 | *You will keep in perfect peace all who trust in you, all whose thoughts are fixed on you!*

Faith in God frees you from the pressures, priorities, and perspectives of this world. It brings peace of mind and heart because it links you to God's peace and power. Faith that God is sovereign gives you the peaceful assurance that he is still in control.

ROMANS 8:5 | *Those who are dominated by the sinful nature think about sinful things, but those who are controlled by the Holy Spirit think about things that please the Spirit.*

GALATIANS 5:22 | *The Holy Spirit produces this kind of fruit in our lives: love, joy, peace, patience, kindness, goodness, faithfulness.*

Faith is inviting God's Holy Spirit to live in you. It is not just an act of the mind; it also taps you into the very resources of God so that you have the power to live in an entirely new way. If God himself is living within you, your life should be dramatically changed.

Promise from God ACTS 16:31 | *Believe in the Lord Jesus and you will be saved.*

FEAR

What should I do when I am fearful?

PSALM 46:1-2 | *God is our refuge and strength, always ready to help in times of trouble. So we will not fear when earthquakes come and the mountains crumble into the sea.*

Remind yourself that God is greater than the most severe threats in life. You will not be surprised by trouble if you recognize how sin has corrupted this world and if you remember he promises to always help when you ask.

DEUTERONOMY 31:6 | *Be strong and courageous! Do not be afraid and do not panic . . . for the LORD your God will personally go ahead of you. He will neither fail you nor abandon you.*

JOHN 14:27 | *I am leaving you with a gift—peace of mind and heart. And the peace I give is a gift the world cannot give. So don't be troubled or afraid.*

Remind yourself that God is always with you. Your situation may be genuinely threatening, but God has not abandoned you and he promises to stay with you. Even if your situation is so bad that it results in death, God has not left you but has instead ushered you into his very presence.

2 TIMOTHY 1:7 | *God has not given us a spirit of fear and timidity, but of power, love, and self-discipline.*

Whatever makes you afraid is an opportunity for you to develop greater faith as you call upon the power of God to help you through your trouble.

GENESIS 26:7 | *[Jacob] was afraid to say, "She is my wife." He thought, "They will kill me to get her."*

Fear must not keep you from doing and saying the things you know are right.

JOSHUA 17:16 | *The Canaanites . . . have iron chariots. . . . They are too strong for us.*

You are not meant to live in fear, not when you are in relationship with an all-powerful God.

What does it mean to fear God?

PSALM 33:8 | *Let the whole world fear the LORD, and let everyone stand in awe of him.*

PROVERBS 9:10 | *Fear of the LORD is the foundation of wisdom.*

Fearing God is not the same as being afraid of God. Being afraid of someone drives you away from him or her. Fearing God means being awed by his power and goodness. This draws you closer to him and to the blessings he gives. A healthy fear should drive you to God for forgiveness and help you keep your perspective about where you need to be in your relationship with him.

How can fearing God make me joyful?

PSALM 2:11 | *Serve the LORD with reverent fear, and rejoice with trembling.*

PSALM 128:1 | *How joyful are those who fear the LORD—all who follow his ways!*

A healthy fear of God recognizes what he could do if he gave you what you deserved. But rejoice, instead, that he gives you mercy and forgiveness. You fear God because of his awesome power; you love God for the way he blesses you with it. And this brings great joy.

What can I learn from fear?

JOSHUA 1:9 | *[The Lord said to Joshua,] "This is my command— be strong and courageous! Do not be afraid or discouraged. For the LORD your God is with you wherever you go."*

Fear can be good if it teaches you about courage. Joshua couldn't have truly understood courage if he hadn't experienced fear. Fear gave him courageous character and taught him to rely on and trust in God.

Promise from God ISAIAH 41:10 | *Don't be afraid, for I am with you. Don't be discouraged, for I am your God. I will strengthen you and help you. I will hold you up with my victorious right hand.*

FORGIVENESS

What does it really mean to be forgiven?

ISAIAH 1:18 | *The LORD [said,] "Though your sins are like scarlet, I will make them as white as snow. Though they are red like crimson, I will make them as white as wool."*

COLOSSIANS 1:22 | *You are holy and blameless as you stand before him without a single fault.*

Forgiveness means that God looks at you as though you have never sinned. When you receive his forgiveness, you are blameless before him. When God forgives, he doesn't sweep your sins under the carpet; instead, he completely washes them away.

Is there a limit to how much God will forgive me?

NUMBERS 14:18 | *The LORD is slow to anger and filled with unfailing love, forgiving every kind of sin and rebellion.*

PSALM 65:3 | *Though we are overwhelmed by our sins, you forgave them all.*

No matter how sinful and disobedient you have been, you can receive God's forgiveness by turning to him in repentance.

PSALM 86:5 | *O Lord, you are so good, so ready to forgive, so full of unfailing love for all who ask for your help.*

EZEKIEL 18:22 | *All their past sins will be forgotten, and they will live because of the righteous things they have done.*

God is ready right now to forgive you.

MATTHEW 18:23-25, 27 | *The Kingdom of Heaven can be compared to a king who decided to bring his accounts up to date. . . . One of his debtors was brought in who owed him millions of dollars. He couldn't pay. . . . Then his master was filled with pity for him, and he released him and forgave his debt.*

God is merciful toward you, even though your debt is great.

LUKE 24:47 | *There is forgiveness of sins for all who repent.*

EPHESIANS 1:7 | *[God] is so rich in kindness and grace that he purchased our freedom with the blood of his Son and forgave our sins.*

COLOSSIANS 1:13-14 | *[God] has rescued us from the kingdom of darkness and transferred us into the Kingdom of his dear Son, who purchased our freedom and forgave our sins.*

God is willing to forgive every sin because Christ has already paid the penalty for all sin by his death.

MARK 3:29 | *Anyone who blasphemes the Holy Spirit will never be forgiven. This is a sin with eternal consequences.*

Those who harden themselves against God's Spirit and reject him utterly will never experience his forgiveness.

Do I have to forgive those who hurt me?

MATTHEW 6:14-15 | *If you forgive those who sin against you, your heavenly Father will forgive you. But if you refuse to forgive others, your Father will not forgive your sins.*

MARK 11:25 | *When you are praying, first forgive anyone you are holding a grudge against, so that your Father in heaven will forgive your sins, too.*

You will receive God's forgiveness only when you forgive others who have wronged you. Being unwilling to forgive shows that you have not understood or benefited from God's forgiveness.

MATTHEW 18:21-22 | *Peter . . . asked, "Lord, how often should I forgive someone who sins against me? Seven times?" "No, not seven times," Jesus replied, "but seventy times seven!"*

Just as God forgives you without limit, you should forgive others without counting how many times.

LUKE 23:34 | *Jesus said, "Father, forgive them, for they don't know what they are doing."*

Jesus forgave even those who mocked and killed him. Be more concerned about your offenders and their relationship with God and less about nursing your own grudges and self-pity.

COLOSSIANS 3:13 | *Make allowance for each other's faults, and forgive anyone who offends you. Remember, the Lord forgave you, so you must forgive others.*

1 PETER 3:9 | *Don't repay evil for evil. Don't retaliate with insults when people insult you. Instead, pay them back with a blessing. That is what God has called you to do, and he will bless you for it.*

When people say hurtful things about you, God wants you to respond by blessing them.

Is it really possible for me to get a fresh start?

2 CORINTHIANS 5:17 | *Anyone who belongs to Christ has become a new person. The old life is gone; a new life has begun!*

Do you have times when you long for a fresh start? God promises that when you place your faith in Jesus, you get a new beginning because his forgiveness washes your sins away, giving you a clean heart before God. Then God promises to put his Holy Spirit in your clean heart and give you the strength, power, and wisdom to live the way God created you to live. And when you mess up, God's forgiveness always provides the opportunity to begin again—any day, any time.

Promise from God 1 JOHN 1:9 | *If we confess our sins to him, he is faithful and just to forgive us our sins and to cleanse us from all wickedness.*

FRIENDSHIP

Can I truly be friends with God?

GENESIS 5:23-24 | *Enoch lived 365 years, walking in close fellowship with God.*

EXODUS 33:11 | *The LORD would speak to Moses face to face, as one speaks to a friend.*

PSALM 25:14 | *The LORD is a friend to those who fear him. He teaches them his covenant.*

God saw Enoch and Moses as his friends. As you develop your relationship with God, you develop a friendship with him. He is your Lord, but he also desires to be your friend.

What is the mark of true friendship?

1 SAMUEL 18:1, 3-4 | *After David had finished talking with Saul, he met Jonathan, the king's son. There was an immediate bond between them. . . . Jonathan made a solemn pact with David, because he loved him as he loved himself. Jonathan sealed the pact by taking off his robe and giving it to David, together with his tunic, sword, bow, and belt.*

PROVERBS 17:17 | *A friend is always loyal, and a brother is born to help in time of need.*

Some friendships are fleeting, and some are lasting. True friendships are glued together with bonds of loyalty and commitment. They remain intact, despite changing external circumstances.

What do I do when I'm having trouble making or keeping friends?

JOB 19:19 | *My close friends detest me. Those I loved have turned against me.*

JOHN 5:7 | *The sick man said, "I have no one to put me into the pool."*

Everyone goes through times when it seems their friends have deserted them. Examine your relationships to make sure you are not causing the breach.

MATTHEW 7:12 | *Do to others whatever you would like them to do to you.*

Everyone wants to have good friends, but few are willing to invest the time and effort necessary to build such relationships. You may not make friends quickly and easily, but you can build strong, lasting friendships over time. It might help you to consider the qualities you desire in a good friend—then work to develop those qualities in your own life.

JOHN 15:15 | *[Jesus said,] "I no longer call you slaves. . . . Now you are my friends, since I have told you everything the Father told me."*

HEBREWS 13:5 | *God has said, "I will never fail you. I will never abandon you."*

Remember that God is your constant friend and will never leave you. Keep showing God's love to others, and they will be drawn to you.

EPHESIANS 4:32 | *Be kind to each other, tenderhearted, forgiving one another, just as God through Christ has forgiven you.*

Acts of kindness and generosity attract others to you.

Male/female friendships involve unique pressures and temptations. Does the Bible offer any guidelines for male/female friendships?

1 CORINTHIANS 13:4-5, 7 | *Love is patient and kind. Love is not jealous. . . . It does not demand its own way. . . . Love never gives up, never loses faith, is always hopeful, and endures through every circumstance.*

This timeless description of Christian love becomes the standard of respect and conduct that should mark all relationships.

ACTS 16:15 | *[Lydia] was baptized along with other members of her household, and she asked us to be her guests. "If you agree that I am a true believer in the Lord," she said, "come and stay at my home." And she urged us until we agreed.*

ACTS 18:18 | *Paul . . . said good-bye to the brothers and sisters. . . . Then he set sail for Syria, taking Priscilla and Aquila with him.*

1 TIMOTHY 5:1-2 | *Talk to younger men as you would to your own brothers. . . . Treat younger women with all purity as you would your own sisters.*

Opposite-sex friendships are valuable, especially since it's important that the person you marry be your friend. The best way to keep your friendships pure is to treat your friends like brothers and sisters. Paul gave women such as Lydia and Priscilla this kind of respect. You can do the same by training yourself to focus on who people really are, not what they look like or what they can do for you. And as a Christian, you have a responsibility to encourage your friends to grow closer to Christ regardless of their gender.

MATTHEW 5:28 | *Anyone who even looks at a woman with lust has already committed adultery with her in his heart.*

EPHESIANS 5:3, 18 | *Let there be no sexual immorality, impurity, or greed among you. . . . Instead, be filled with the Holy Spirit.*

In dramatic contrast to much that you see in your culture, Jesus calls you to a standard of sexual purity in thought as well as in action.

What gets in the way of friendships?

1 SAMUEL 18:9-11 | *Saul kept a jealous eye on David. . . . Saul had a spear in his hand, and he suddenly hurled it at David.*

Jealousy is a great dividing force of friendships. Envy of what a friend has will soon turn to anger and bitterness, causing you to separate yourself from the one you truly cared for.

PSALM 41:9 | *Even my best friend, the one I trusted completely . . . has turned against me.*

When trust is seriously damaged, even the closest friendship is at risk.

2 SAMUEL 13:11 | *As [Tamar] was feeding [Amnon], he grabbed her and demanded, "Come to bed with me."*

Friendships are destroyed when boundaries are violated.

Promise from God MATTHEW 18:20 | *[Jesus said,] "Where two or three gather together as my followers, I am there among them."*

FUN

Can I be a Christian and still have fun?

NEHEMIAH 8:10 | *Go and celebrate with a feast . . . and share gifts of food with people who have nothing prepared. This is a sacred day before our Lord. Don't be dejected and sad, for the joy of the LORD is your strength!*

PROVERBS 13:9 | *The life of the godly is full of light and joy, but the light of the wicked will be snuffed out.*

MATTHEW 25:21 | *You have been faithful. . . . Let's celebrate together!*

Joy, fun, and celebration, as God intended, are important parts of Christian faith because they lift your spirits and help you see the beauty and meaning in life. Good times on earth are a taste of heaven.

What kinds of fun are inappropriate?

1 PETER 4:3 | *You have had enough in the past of the evil things that godless people enjoy—their immorality and lust, their feasting and drunkenness and wild parties, and their terrible worship of idols.*

Fun is wrong when it is self-centered or indulgent, when it involves sinful acts, when it can tempt you into sin, or when it is hurtful to others.

Promise from God ECCLESIASTES 11:9 | *Young people, it's wonderful to be young! Enjoy every minute of it. Do everything you want to do; take it all in. But remember that you must give an account to God for everything you do.*

GIVING

Why should I give?

MALACHI 3:10 | *"Bring all the tithes into the storehouse so there will be enough food in my Temple. If you do," says the LORD of Heaven's Armies, "I will open the windows of heaven for you. I will pour out a blessing so great you won't have enough room to take it in! Try it! Put me to the test!"*

When you give, your thoughts and actions shift away from yourself (which is self-centered) and toward others (which demonstrates love and care).

LUKE 21:3 | *"I tell you the truth," Jesus said, "this poor widow has given more than all the rest of [the rich people]."*

JOHN 3:16 | *God loved the world so much that he gave his one and only Son.*

You should give to learn the power of, and to model, the sacrificial giving of God.

EXODUS 23:19 | *As you harvest your crops, bring the very best of the first harvest to the house of the LORD your God.*

You should give first to God because it demonstrates that he is first in your life.

1 CHRONICLES 29:14 | *Everything we have has come from you, and we give you only what you first gave us!*

You should give because it reminds you that what you own is a gift from God.

2 CORINTHIANS 9:11 | *When we take your gifts to those who need them, they will thank God.*

You should give to others so that God will be glorified.

1 PETER 4:10 | *God has given each of you a gift from his great variety of spiritual gifts. Use them well to serve one another.*

The more you give of yourself, the more God's generosity flows through you.

LUKE 6:38 | *Give, and you will receive. Your gift will return to you in full—pressed down, shaken together to make room for more, running over, and poured into your lap.*

2 CORINTHIANS 9:6 | *Remember this—a farmer who plants only a few seeds will get a small crop. But the one who plants generously will get a generous crop.*

You should not give so that you will be given to, but your resources often grow as you give more. One of the reasons this occurs is that the qualities that make you generous also make you responsible and trustworthy. But another important reason is that God, in his grace, may entrust more to you so that you will be a bigger channel of his blessing in this world.

How much should I give?

DEUTERONOMY 14:22 | *You must set aside a tithe of your crops— one-tenth of all the crops you harvest each year.*

1 CORINTHIANS 16:2 | *On the first day of each week, you should each put aside a portion of the money you have earned.*

2 CORINTHIANS 9:7 | *You must each decide in your heart how much to give. And don't give reluctantly or in response to pressure. "For God loves a person who gives cheerfully."*

While the Old Testament specifically talks about giving one-tenth of what you earn to God, the New Testament encourages you to give what you can, to give sacrificially, and to give with a grateful and generous heart. For many, this will mean giving far more than one-tenth!

Promise from God LUKE 6:38 | *Give, and you will receive. Your gift will return to you in full—pressed down, shaken together to make room for more, running over, and poured into your lap. The amount you give will determine the amount you get back.*

GOSSIP

Why is gossip so bad?

JAMES 1:26 | *If you claim to be religious but don't control your tongue, you are fooling yourself, and your religion is worthless.*

What comes out of your mouth shows what is in your heart. Gossip, criticism, flattery, lies, and profanity are not only "word" problems but "heart" problems as well.

PROVERBS 11:13 | *A gossip goes around telling secrets, but those who are trustworthy can keep a confidence.*

Gossips make poor friends. Gossips are demolition experts, trying to tear others down, while trustworthy people build others up.

ROMANS 1:29 | *Their lives became full of every kind of wickedness, sin, greed, hate, envy, murder, quarreling, deception, malicious behavior, and gossip.*

God catalogs gossip with such sins as greed, hate, envy, and murder.

1 TIMOTHY 5:13 | *If they are on the list [for support], [the younger widows] will learn to be lazy and will spend their time gossiping from house to house, meddling in other people's business and talking about things they shouldn't.*

Gossiping often grows out of idleness. You have nothing better to do than sit around talking about other people. Then you wind up saying things you later regret.

PROVERBS 18:8 | *Rumors are dainty morsels that sink deep into one's heart.*

Gossip hurts others. It also destroys your credibility if the gossip proves false.

How do I stop gossip?

PROVERBS 26:20 | *Fire goes out without wood, and quarrels disappear when gossip stops.*

Stop the chain of gossip with you! When you hear gossip, you can do something about it—you can decide not to spread it any further.

DEUTERONOMY 13:14 | *You must examine the facts carefully.*

If you are concerned about something you've heard, look carefully into the matter without assuming that what you have been told is true. Go to the source and get the facts straight.

EPHESIANS 4:29 | *Let everything you say be good and helpful, so that your words will be an encouragement to those who hear them.*

It's really true—what you spend most of your time thinking about is what you end up doing. When you're tempted to complain, train yourself instead to pray. When you're tempted to gossip, compliment or encourage someone instead.

COLOSSIANS 3:17 | *Whatever you do or say, do it as a representative of the Lord Jesus.*

If you think you may be about to gossip, ask yourself, "Does the person I'm talking to need to know this? Is it true, accurate, and helpful?"

Promise from God 1 PETER 3:10 | *If you want to enjoy life and see many happy days, keep your tongue from speaking evil and your lips from telling lies.*

GRACE

What is grace?

ROMANS 6:23 | *The wages of sin is death, but the free gift of God is eternal life through Christ Jesus our Lord.*

EPHESIANS 2:8-9 | *God saved you by his grace when you believed. And you can't take credit for this; it is a gift from God. Salvation is not a reward for the good things we have done, so none of us can boast about it.*

Grace is a big favor done for someone without expecting anything in return. When the Bible says you are saved by grace, it means that God has done you the biggest favor of all—he has pardoned you from the death sentence you deserve for rebelling against him. By grace, you are forgiven for your sin and restored to full fellowship with God. Like the gift of life itself, you cannot take credit for it—any more than a baby can brag about being born! The only hitch to grace is that you must accept it as a gift; otherwise you can't enjoy its benefits.

How does grace affect my daily life?

ROMANS 6:14 | *Sin is no longer your master, for you no longer live under the requirements of the law. Instead, you live under the freedom of God's grace.*

God's grace provides forgiveness for your sin and breaks its power over your life. The Holy Spirit gives you the desire to please God and the spiritual wisdom to be able to discern the truth and pursue it.

How does grace affect my view of God?

PSALM 103:8 | *The LORD is compassionate and merciful, slow to get angry and filled with unfailing love.*

If you believe God is always angry with you, you will be fearful of him or defensive and antagonistic toward him. When you understand the depth of his love for you and his grace toward you, you will live with the joy of being forgiven and the knowledge that you will live forever in heaven. You no longer fear God's retribution but can freely pursue a relationship with him.

Promise from God ROMANS 6:14 | *Sin is no longer your master, for you no longer live under the requirements of the law. Instead, you live under the freedom of God's grace.*

GUIDANCE

Will God tell me what he wants me to do for the rest of my life?

PSALM 119:105 | *Your word is a lamp to guide my feet and a light for my path.*

PSALM 138:8 | *The LORD will work out his plans for my life— for your faithful love, O LORD, endures forever.*

ISAIAH 30:21 | *Your own ears will hear him. Right behind you a voice will say, "This is the way you should go," whether to the right or to the left.*

If you could see your future, you'd either be very scared of the hard times ahead or get very cocky about your accomplishments. Instead of a searchlight that brightens a huge area, God's guidance is more like a flashlight that illuminates just enough of the path ahead to show you where to take the next few steps. God usually doesn't reveal it all at once. He wants you to learn to trust him each step of the way.

Promise from God PSALM 32:8 | *The LORD says, "I will guide you along the best pathway for your life. I will advise you and watch over you."*

HABITS

What are some of the bad habits the Bible talks about?

1 JOHN 3:8 | *When people keep on sinning, it shows that they belong to the devil, who has been sinning since the beginning.*

Sinning is a habit you cannot completely stop, but a pattern of sinful living with no change in behavior shows that you are not serious about following God.

NUMBERS 11:1 | *The people began to complain about their hardship.*

The Israelites developed a bad habit of complaining. Chronic complaining can quickly turn into bitterness.

1 TIMOTHY 5:13 | *They will learn to be lazy and will spend their time gossiping.*

Having too much time and too little to do can be fertile ground for bad habits. Idleness makes it easy to develop the bad habit of gossiping.

How can God help me deal with bad habits?

1 JOHN 2:15 | *Do not love this world nor the things it offers you.*

Sin often appears lovely and attractive. In the same way, indulging in bad habits often feels good even though you know they are bad for you. Breaking a bad habit can be hard because you are losing something you enjoy. Understand that there may be a grieving process, but losing a bad habit ultimately brings a deeper satisfaction from doing what is pleasing to God.

ROMANS 7:15, 25 | *[Paul said,] "I don't really understand myself, for I want to do what is right, but I don't do it. Instead, I do what I hate. . . . The answer is in Jesus Christ."*

One of the best ways to deal with bad habits is to recognize them for what they are and confess them honestly. Paul knew that he could not kick the habit of sin completely. But he did know that, with God's help, he could make progress every day. You may have to give up a habit in phases, one step at a time.

COLOSSIANS 3:2 | *Think about the things of heaven, not the things of earth.*

It will be much easier to break bad habits if you replace them with good habits, which you can learn from studying Jesus' life.

How can I develop good habits?

HEBREWS 10:25 | *Let us not neglect our meeting together, as some people do, but encourage one another, especially now that the day of his return is drawing near.*

Meeting with other believers is a good habit because it provides necessary support and fellowship, it enriches you as you search God's Word together, it keeps you busy when you might otherwise be slipping into bad habits, and it offers accountability.

GENESIS 26:21-22 | *Isaac's men then dug another well, but again there was a dispute over it. . . . Abandoning that one, Isaac moved on and dug another well. This time there was no dispute over it.*

Isaac pursued a habit of living in peace. In this case, it meant staying away from the source of the conflict, the Philistines, even at great personal cost.

PSALM 28:7 | *The LORD is my strength and shield. I trust him with all my heart. He helps me, and my heart is filled with joy. I burst out in songs of thanksgiving.*

As a young boy, David developed the habits of talking to God, singing praises to him, and writing psalms. These helped him to trust in and follow God all his life.

Promise from God ROMANS 8:5 | *Those who are dominated by the sinful nature think about sinful things, but those who are controlled by the Holy Spirit think about things that please the Spirit.*

HEAVEN

Is there really a heaven?

JOHN 14:2 | *[Jesus said,] "There is more than enough room in my Father's home. If this were not so, would I have told you that I am going to prepare a place for you?"*

2 CORINTHIANS 5:1 | *We know that when this earthly tent we live in is taken down (that is, when we die and leave this earthly body), we will have a house in heaven.*

Not only is there a heaven, but Jesus is making preparations for your arrival. Heaven is described most often in terms of being your home. It is not a paradise you will simply visit on vacation, but an eternal dwelling place where you will live in joyful fellowship with your heavenly Father and his family.

ECCLESIASTES 3:11 | *God has made everything beautiful for its own time. He has planted eternity in the human heart.*

God created you with an instinct for heaven, an inner longing to live forever. It is not just wishful thinking; it is God's intended purpose for you.

1 CORINTHIANS 15:20 | *Christ has been raised from the dead. He is the first of a great harvest of all who have died.*

Jesus' resurrection gives you the promise and assurance of your own resurrection to heaven and eternal life.

GENESIS 1:1, 9, 11, 20, 24, 27, 31 | *In the beginning God created the heavens and the earth. . . . Then God said, "Let the waters beneath the sky flow together into one place, so dry ground may appear.". . . Then God said, "Let the land sprout with vegetation—every sort of seed-bearing plant, and trees.". . . Then God said, "Let the waters swarm with fish and other life. Let the skies be filled with birds of every kind.". . . Then God said, "Let the earth produce every sort of animal.". . . [Then] God created human beings in his own image . . . male and female he created them. . . . Then God looked over all he had made, and he saw that it was very good!*

2 PETER 3:13 | *We are looking forward to the new heavens and new earth [God] has promised, a world filled with God's righteousness.*

REVELATION 21:1 | *I saw a new heaven and a new earth.*

God originally created earth to be heaven—the place where he would live with people and walk and talk with them, side by side. Sin changed all that when it separated Adam and Eve from God and corrupted the earth. But the point is that God originally thought of heavenly paradise as a very physical place, with trees and plants, mountains and waterfalls, fruits and vegetables. The Bible consistently refers to the new heaven—the place where we will be reunited with God—and a new earth. The place where we will live forever with God will be very similar to the place where we live now. If God said the original earth he created was "very good," then the new earth he is preparing for us will be similar and familiar to us.

What is heaven like?

ISAIAH 65:17 | *[The sovereign Lord said,] "Look! I am creating new heavens and a new earth, and no one will even think about the old ones anymore."*

PHILIPPIANS 3:21 | *[The Lord Jesus Christ] will take our weak mortal bodies and change them into glorious bodies like his own, using the same power with which he will bring everything under his control.*

JAMES 1:17 | *Whatever is good and perfect comes down to us from God our Father, who created all the lights in the heavens.*

REVELATION 21:3-4 | *I heard a loud shout from the throne, saying, "Look, God's home is now among his people! He will live with them, and they will be his people. God himself will be with them. He will wipe every tear from their eyes, and there will be no more death or sorrow or crying or pain. All these things are gone forever."*

REVELATION 22:5 | *There will be no night there—no need for lamps or sun—for the Lord God will shine on [his servants]. And they will reign forever and ever.*

In heaven we will live forever with God. There will be no sadness, no pain, no evil, no death. Everything will be perfect and glorious. God will give you a new body, and you will be able to talk face-to-face with the Lord himself.

Who will get into heaven?

MATTHEW 5:3 | *God blesses those who are poor and realize their need for him, for the Kingdom of Heaven is theirs.*

MATTHEW 19:14 | *Jesus said, "Let the children come to me. Don't stop them! For the Kingdom of Heaven belongs to those who are like these children."*

JOHN 3:16 | *God loved the world so much that he gave his one and only Son, so that everyone who believes in him will not perish but have eternal life.*

Those who have a relationship with Jesus Christ and believe that he alone is God will enter heaven. When you know Jesus and accept that only he can forgive sin (the one thing that separates you from God), you are guaranteed entrance into heaven.

Does the Bible really claim that there is only one way to heaven?

JOHN 14:6 | *Jesus [said], "I am the way, the truth, and the life. No one can come to the Father except through me."*

Jesus is the only way to heaven. You may want to buy your way in, work your way in, think your way in. But the Bible is clear—Jesus Christ provides the only way in. Believing in him, gratefully accepting his offer of salvation, is the only way to get to life's most important destination.

Promise from God 1 CORINTHIANS 2:9 | *No eye has seen, no ear has heard, and no mind has imagined what God has prepared for those who love him.*

HELL

Is there really a place called hell?

MATTHEW 7:13 | *You can enter God's Kingdom only through the narrow gate. The highway to hell is broad, and its gate is wide for the many who choose that way.*

MATTHEW 13:49-50 | *At the end of the world . . . the angels will come and separate the wicked people from the righteous, throwing the wicked into the fiery furnace, where there will be weeping and gnashing of teeth.*

2 PETER 2:4 | *God did not spare even the angels who sinned. He threw them into hell, in gloomy pits of darkness, where they are being held until the day of judgment.*

REVELATION 20:10 | *The devil . . . was thrown into the fiery lake of burning sulfur, joining the beast and the false prophet. There they will be tormented day and night forever and ever.*

The Bible leaves no doubt that hell is a very real place. If there weren't a real hell, then Jesus' death and resurrection to save us from sin's consequences would be meaningless.

What is hell like?

LUKE 16:22-24 | *[Lazarus] died and was carried by the angels to be with Abraham. The rich man also died and was buried, and his soul went to the place of the dead. There, in torment, he saw Abraham in the far distance with Lazarus at his side. The rich man shouted, "Father Abraham, have some pity! Send Lazarus over here to dip the tip of his finger in water and cool my tongue. I am in anguish in these flames."*

2 PETER 2:4 | *God did not spare even the angels who sinned. He threw them into hell, in gloomy pits of darkness, where they are being held until the day of judgment.*

JUDE 1:7 | *Those cities [Sodom and Gomorrah] were destroyed by fire and serve as a warning of the eternal fire of God's judgment.*

REVELATION 19:20 | *Both the beast and his false prophet were thrown alive into the fiery lake of burning sulfur.*

The Bible compares hell to existence in a burning fire, a dark and gloomy place where everyone is forever separated from God and all that is good. Some people think hell will be fun, like a never-ending, raunchy party. On the contrary, it seems that the Bible alludes to hell as a lonely place, where its people are isolated from relationships. Furthermore, here on earth people tend to think in time spans that have a beginning and an end, but there will be no end to hell.

How can I be assured that I am not going to hell?

JOHN 3:16 | *God loved the world so much that he gave his one and only Son, so that everyone who believes in him will not perish but have eternal life.*

JOHN 14:6 | *Jesus [said], "I am the way, the truth, and the life. No one can come to the Father except through me."*

ROMANS 10:9 | *If you confess with your mouth that Jesus is Lord and believe in your heart that God raised him from the dead, you will be saved.*

1 JOHN 4:17 | *As we live in God, our love grows more perfect. So we will not be afraid on the day of judgment, but we can face him with confidence because we live like Jesus here in this world.*

There is only one way to be certain that you will not go to hell. You must confess your sin to Jesus and believe in him as your personal Savior. By taking this step, you secure your place in heaven, and you no longer have to fear hell.

Promise from God   MATTHEW 7:13 | *You can enter God's Kingdom only through the narrow gate. The highway to hell is broad, and its gate is wide for the many who choose that way.*

HOMOSEXUALITY

Is homosexuality wrong?

GENESIS 2:18, 21-24 | *The LORD God said, "It is not good for the man to be alone. I will make a helper who is just right for him." . . . So the LORD God caused the man to fall into a deep sleep. While the man slept, the LORD God took out one of the man's ribs and closed up the opening. Then the LORD God made a woman from the rib, and he brought her to the man. "At last!" the man exclaimed. "This one is bone from my bone, and flesh from my flesh! She will be called 'woman,' because she was taken from 'man.'" This explains why a man leaves his father and mother and is joined to his wife, and the two are united into one.*

LEVITICUS 18:22 | *Do not practice homosexuality, having sex with another man as with a woman. It is a detestable sin.*

God views the practice of homosexuality as sin because it violates the boundaries of sexual relationships that he established and because it violates the covenant of marriage between a man and a woman, which he also established. At the very beginning of time, God created the perfect union, a man and a woman. God, as the Creator of men and women, has both male and female characteristics. When a man and woman come together in marriage, they represent, or symbolize, the unity of these characteristics that are all found in God.

Are people born homosexual?

LEVITICUS 20:13 | *If a man practices homosexuality, having sex with another man as with a woman, both men have committed a detestable act. They must both be put to death, for they are guilty of a capital offense.*

It would be contrary to God's character for him to create a person to be homosexual when his laws call it a sin. However, can a person be born with a disposition toward homosexuality? Can a person be born with a disposition to alcoholism or some other addiction? Yes. In fact, all people are born with a disposition to sin and to certain sins in particular, because everyone is born with a sinful nature. Different people have a disposition to different sinful behaviors. But although everyone is born with a disposition to sin, it doesn't make sin right. God didn't create sinners, nor does he condone sin. He wants you to live in obedience to him.

How can a person overcome homosexual feelings?

1 CORINTHIANS 10:13 | *The temptations in your life are no different from what others experience. And God is faithful. He will not allow the temptation to be more than you can stand. When you are tempted, he will show you a way out so that you can endure.*

JAMES 1:12 | *God blesses those who patiently endure testing and temptation. Afterward they will receive the crown of life that God has promised to those who love him.*

JAMES 4:17 | *Remember, it is sin to know what you ought to do and then not do it.*

A person can overcome homosexual feelings in the same way that a person can overcome any sinful temptation—by looking to God for help, resolving to stand firm, and avoiding tempting situations.

Can God forgive homosexual behavior?

HEBREWS 4:16 | *Let us come boldly to the throne of our gracious God. There we will receive his mercy, and we will find grace to help us when we need it most.*

HEBREWS 8:12 | *[The Lord said,] "I will forgive their wickedness, and I will never again remember their sins."*

1 JOHN 1:9 | *If we confess our sins to him, he is faithful and just to forgive us our sins and to cleanse us from all wickedness.*

God will forgive any sin that you sincerely confess to him. When you confess your sin to God, he not only forgives you but gives you a new outlook on life. He will change your heart and make you a new person, free from the imprisonment of your past sins.

Promise from God HEBREWS 4:16 | *Let us come boldly to the throne of our gracious God. There we will receive his mercy, and we will find grace to help us when we need it most.*

HONESTY

Why is it so important to be honest?

PSALM 24:3-4 | *Who may climb the mountain of the LORD? Who may stand in his holy place? Only those whose hands and hearts are pure . . . and never tell lies.*

Walking with God requires honesty because honesty shows purity, integrity, and a desire to do what is true and right.

MATTHEW 12:33 | *A tree is identified by its fruit. If a tree is good, its fruit will be good.*

LUKE 16:10 | *If you are dishonest in little things, you won't be honest with greater responsibilities.*

Your level of honesty demonstrates the quality of your character.

1 TIMOTHY 1:19 | *Cling to your faith in Christ, and keep your conscience clear. For some people have deliberately violated their consciences; as a result, their faith has been shipwrecked.*

Honesty brings a clear conscience.

DEUTERONOMY 25:13-15 | *You must use accurate scales when you weigh out merchandise, and you must use full and honest measures . . . so that you may enjoy a long life.*

Dishonesty and deception are forms of bondage because they are needed to hide selfish motives. Honesty brings freedom from guilt and from the consequences of deceptive actions.

2 KINGS 22:7 | *Don't require the construction supervisors to keep account of the money they receive, for they are honest and trustworthy men.*

Striving for honesty helps you develop a reputation of integrity. Consistent honesty in the past and the present builds trust for continued honesty in the future.

PSALM 37:37 | *Look at those who are honest and good, for a wonderful future awaits those who love peace.*

Striving for honesty helps you to enjoy life because you can live at peace with God and yourself.

Does honesty mean always telling everything I know?

PROVERBS 29:20 | *There is more hope for a fool than for someone who speaks without thinking.*

ECCLESIASTES 3:1, 7 | *For everything there is a season, a time for every activity under heaven. . . . A time to be quiet and a time to speak.*

COLOSSIANS 4:6 | *Let your conversation be gracious and attractive so that you will have the right response for everyone.*

Honesty should not be confused with gossip. Just because you know something doesn't mean you have to tell everyone about it. Honesty also involves integrity, making sure that what you say is helpful and builds others up rather than tears them down. The person who thinks before speaking is wise. It is not deceitful to withhold information that others don't need to know unless, of course, you are under oath in a court of law.

Promise from God PROVERBS 12:19 | *Truthful words stand the test of time, but lies are soon exposed.*

HOPE

What can I do when my situation seems hopeless?

1 SAMUEL 1:10 | *Hannah was in deep anguish, crying bitterly as she prayed to the LORD.*

You can pray. In the midst of Hannah's hopelessness, she prayed to God, knowing that if any hope were to be found, it would be found in him.

ACTS 16:24-25 | *The jailer put them into the inner dungeon and clamped their feet in the stocks. Around midnight Paul and Silas were praying and singing hymns to God, and the other prisoners were listening.*

You can worship. Paul and Silas were on death row for preaching about Jesus, yet in this hopeless situation they sang praises to God. Why? Because of their hope in God's promises.

PROVERBS 10:28 | *The hopes of the godly result in happiness, but the expectations of the wicked come to nothing.*

You can focus on eternity. No matter how hopeless things seem here on earth, in Jesus you have ultimate, eternal hope. Because you know him, you have been promised a joyful eternal future in heaven. There is much more living to do beyond the grave.

How do I put my hope in God?

PHILIPPIANS 3:13-14 | *Forgetting the past and looking forward to what lies ahead, I press on to reach the end of the race and receive the heavenly prize for which God, through Christ Jesus, is calling us.*

Hope involves an understanding of the future. And even here on earth God's plans are to bless, not hurt you. So if you follow his plans for you, you can look forward to your future with joyful anticipation.

ROMANS 8:24 | *We were given this hope when we were saved. (If we already have something, we don't need to hope for it.)*

Hope, by definition, is expecting something that has not yet occurred. Once hope is fulfilled, it isn't hope anymore. Thus, an important part of hope is waiting patiently for God to work.

HEBREWS 11:1 | *Faith is the confidence that what we hope for will actually happen; it gives us assurance about things we cannot see.*

Have faith in God to do what he has promised, and trust that he will. Your hopes are not idle hopes because they are built on the solid foundation of his trustworthiness.

Promises from God   PSALM 71:5 | *O Lord, you alone are my hope.*

JEREMIAH 29:11 | *"I know the plans I have for you," says the LORD. "They are plans for good and not for disaster, to give you a future and a hope."*

HUMILITY

What is true humility?

ZEPHANIAH 3:12 | *Those who are left will be the lowly and humble, for it is they who trust in the name of the LORD.*

Humility is not thinking too highly of yourself.

MATTHEW 18:4 | *Anyone who becomes as humble as this little child is the greatest in the Kingdom of Heaven.*

Humility is childlike. It is an attitude of total trust in a great God.

TITUS 3:2 | *[Believers] must not slander anyone and must avoid quarreling. Instead, they should be gentle and show true humility to everyone.*

Humility is truly caring about others and looking out for their best interests.

PROVERBS 12:23 | *The wise don't make a show of their knowledge, but fools broadcast their foolishness.*

Humility is refraining from proving what you know, how good you are at something, or that you are always right.

PROVERBS 13:10 | *Pride leads to conflict; those who take advice are wise.*

Humility allows you to ask for advice.

GENESIS 32:9-10 | *Jacob prayed, "O God . . . you promised me, 'I will treat you kindly.' I am not worthy of all the unfailing love and faithfulness you have shown to me, your servant."*

Humility comes when you recognize your need for God and then acknowledge how he provides for you.

How was Jesus humble?

LUKE 2:6-7 | *The time came for [Mary's] baby to be born. She gave birth to her first child, a son. She wrapped him snugly in strips of cloth and laid him in a manger, because there was no lodging available for them.*

God wanted Jesus to have a humble birth as a sign that his offer of salvation is for everyone, regardless of race or class or socioeconomic position.

ZECHARIAH 9:9 | *Rejoice, O people of Zion! Shout in triumph, O people of Jerusalem! Look, your king is coming to you. He is righteous and victorious, yet he is humble, riding on a donkey—riding on a donkey's colt.*

Jesus was King of kings, yet on his royal ride into Jerusalem, when the crowds proclaimed him king (see Matthew 21:1-11), he sat on a lowly donkey.

HEBREWS 2:9 | *Jesus . . . was given a position "a little lower than the angels"; and because he suffered death for us, he is now "crowned with glory and honor." Yes, by God's grace, Jesus tasted death for everyone.*

Jesus had all the glory and honor of sitting at God's right hand, but for your sake he gave that up to die a criminal's death so that you could be saved from eternal punishment and enjoy eternal life with him.

How can humility help me deal with sin?

JAMES 4:6-10 | *[God] gives us even more grace to stand against such evil desires. As the Scriptures say, "God opposes the proud but favors the humble." So humble yourselves before God. Resist the devil, and he will flee from you. Come close to God, and God will come close to you. Wash your hands, you sinners; purify your hearts, for your loyalty is divided between God and the world. Let there be tears for what you have done. . . . Humble yourselves before the Lord, and he will lift you up in honor.*

Humility is recognizing the sin in your life. Openly admit that you need God, and seek his forgiveness. No proud person can do this.

Promise from God MATTHEW 23:12 | *Those who exalt themselves will be humbled, and those who humble themselves will be exalted.*

JEALOUSY

Why is jealousy so harmful?

PROVERBS 14:30 | *A peaceful heart leads to a healthy body; jealousy is like cancer in the bones.*

Jealousy eats away at you—it causes you to feed on the destructive emotions of anger and bitterness rather than being content with what you have and genuinely happy for the success of others.

1 SAMUEL 18:9-11 | *Saul kept a jealous eye on David. . . . David was playing the harp, as he did each day. But Saul had a spear in his hand, and he suddenly hurled it at David, intending to pin him to the wall.*

ACTS 17:5-6 | *Some of the Jews were jealous, so they gathered some troublemakers from the marketplace to form a mob and start a riot. They attacked the home of Jason, searching for Paul and Silas so they could drag them out to the crowd. Not finding them there, they dragged out Jason and some of the other believers instead.*

Jealousy for attention or affection can drive people to extreme action, even seeking to harm or kill others. Envy and jealousy not only destroy the people who feel them but often lead these people to attack the objects of their envy and jealousy. While you may not attack a person with a spear, as Saul did, you may use sharp words and piercing comments, which can be potentially as damaging.

How can I deal with jealousy?

GENESIS 30:1 | *When Rachel saw that she wasn't having any children for Jacob, she became jealous of her sister.*

Instead of enjoying the favor and love of her husband, Rachel focused on her inability to give Jacob children. She became jealous of her sister, Leah. The cure for jealousy is being thankful and enjoying what you have instead of focusing on what you don't have.

MATTHEW 20:15 | *Should you be jealous because I am kind to others?*

Jealousy reveals selfishness. You want for yourself what someone else has. Rejoicing in another's success or good fortune will eliminate jealousy and increase your own capacity for joy.

JOHN 21:19-22 | *Jesus said this to let [Peter] know by what kind of death he would glorify God. . . . Peter turned around and saw behind them the disciple Jesus loved. . . . Peter asked Jesus, "What about him, Lord?" Jesus replied, "If I want him to remain alive until I return, what is that to you? As for you, follow me."*

When Peter heard Jesus' prophecy of his death, he wondered what would happen to the other disciple (John). Jesus made it clear that Peter was to pay attention to his own concerns, not those of others. In many situations, you may be tempted to compare your lot in life with another's. Instead, keep your focus on what you believe God wants you to do, and accept that his will for you is best.

Promise from God PROVERBS 14:30 | *A peaceful heart leads to a healthy body; jealousy is like cancer in the bones.*

JUDGING OTHERS

What's the difference between judging others and providing constructive criticism?

MATTHEW 7:1-3 | *Do not judge others, and you will not be judged. For you will be treated as you treat others. The standard you use in judging is the standard by which you will be judged. And why worry about a speck in your friend's eye when you have a log in your own?*

COLOSSIANS 3:13 | *Make allowance for each other's faults, and forgive anyone who offends you. Remember, the Lord forgave you, so you must forgive others.*

JAMES 4:11 | *Don't speak evil against each other, dear brothers and sisters. If you criticize and judge each other, then you are criticizing and judging God's law. But your job is to obey the law, not to judge whether it applies to you.*

One coach berates a player publicly for a mistake made in a game. Another coach waits until the game is over and addresses a player privately, with instruction about how to avoid making the same mistake again. While no one likes criticism—even when it is constructive—people sometimes need it. But it is much easier to receive criticism when offered gently and in love rather than harshly and with the intention to humiliate. To judge someone is to criticize with no effort to see that person succeed or improve. To offer constructive criticism is to invest in another for the purposes of helping that person become who God created him or her to be as well as building a relationship.

Promise from God   MATTHEW 7:1 | *Do not judge others, and you will not be judged.*

KNOWLEDGE/LEARNING

Why is knowledge so important?

PROVERBS 1:4 | *These proverbs will give insight to the simple, knowledge and discernment to the young.*

Knowledge leads to purpose. Knowledge of Jesus changes your purpose in life. If you are struggling with knowing what that is, spend time studying and getting to know God's Word; he will reveal to you his purpose for you.

PROVERBS 2:10 | *Wisdom will enter your heart, and knowledge will fill you with joy.*

Using the wisdom God has given you helps you apply what you know and saves you from choosing wrong paths.

How can knowledge be harmful?

ISAIAH 47:10-11 | *You felt secure in your wickedness. "No one sees me," you said. But your "wisdom" and "knowledge" have led you astray, and you said, "I am the only one, and there is no other." So disaster will overtake you, and you won't be able to charm it away.*

Knowledge is harmful when it leads you to think you no longer need God. If you think you can rely on your own smarts to make it through this life, you will be deeply disappointed when you get to the end.

Promise from God   PROVERBS 2:3-5 | *Cry out for insight, and ask for understanding. Search for them as you would for silver; seek them like hidden treasures. Then you will understand what it means to fear the LORD, and you will gain knowledge of God.*

LISTENING

Why is listening so important?

PROVERBS 1:9 | *What you learn from [your father and mother] will crown you with grace and be a chain of honor around your neck.*

Good listening helps you grow and mature. It fosters learning, which leads to knowledge and wisdom.

PROVERBS 5:13-14 | *Oh, why didn't I listen to my teachers? Why didn't I pay attention to my instructors? I have come to the brink of utter ruin, and now I must face public disgrace.*

Listening helps keep you from making mistakes you could have avoided.

PROVERBS 2:1, 9 | *My child, listen to what I say, and treasure my commands. . . . Then you will understand what is right . . . and you will find the right way to go.*

Listening to God is essential to making good decisions. When you truly listen to the Holy Spirit and to God's commands, you will have the guidance you need to make wise choices.

PROVERBS 8:6 | *Listen to me! For I have important things to tell you.*

Listening keeps you from being closed-minded. It allows you to hear a variety of ideas from many different sources.

EXODUS 18:24 | *Moses listened to his father-in-law's advice and followed his suggestions.*

Listening shows that you respect others. It honors their words, and they feel affirmed because you've listened to them.

PROVERBS 21:13 | *Those who shut their ears to the cries of the poor will be ignored in their own time of need.*

Listening is more than hearing; it connects you with others. It helps you know when they are in need and the best way to help them.

What are some things I shouldn't listen to?

GENESIS 3:1, 6 | *[The serpent] asked the woman, "Did God really say you must not eat the fruit from any of the trees in the garden?" . . . She saw that the tree was beautiful and its fruit looked delicious, and she wanted the wisdom it would give her. So she took some of the fruit and ate it.*

MATTHEW 6:13 | *Don't let us yield to temptation.*

Temptation.

LEVITICUS 19:16 | *Do not spread slanderous gossip among your people.*

Gossip.

MARK 13:21-23 | *If anyone tells you, "Look, here is the Messiah," or "There he is," don't believe it. For false messiahs and false prophets will rise up and perform signs and wonders so as to deceive, if possible, even God's chosen ones. Watch out!*

False teaching.

EPHESIANS 5:4 | *Obscene stories, foolish talk, and coarse jokes— these are not for you.*

Foolish talk and off-color stories.

PROVERBS 13:5 | *The godly hate lies.*

Lies.

PROVERBS 29:5 | *To flatter friends is to lay a trap for their feet.*

Flattery.

How can I better listen to God?

PSALM 4:3 | *You can be sure of this: . . . The LORD will answer when I call to him.*

PSALM 5:3 | *Each morning I bring my requests to you and wait expectantly.*

Through prayer. After you talk to God, stay and listen for a while.

PSALM 46:10 | *Be still, and know that I am God!*

Being quiet helps you better hear God's voice. Find times and places where there's nothing else to hear but God's voice.

LUKE 8:18 | *Pay attention to how you hear. To those who listen to my teaching, more understanding will be given. But for those who are not listening, even what they think they understand will be taken away from them.*

When you think you've heard something from God, pay attention to it. Don't miss an opportunity for a lesson from the Master Teacher.

Promise from God PROVERBS 1:23 | *Come and listen to my counsel. I'll share my heart with you and make you wise.*

LONELINESS

Why am I sometimes lonely?

GENESIS 2:18 | *The LORD God said, "It is not good for the man to be alone. I will make a helper who is just right for him."*

God did not intend for you to be lonely. On the contrary, it was God who recognized Adam's need for companionship. He gave Adam the task of naming the animals so that Adam could recognize his own need for a human companion. It was then that God created woman (see Genesis 2:19-22).

1 SAMUEL 20:41 | *David bowed three times to Jonathan. . . . Both of them were in tears as they embraced each other and said good-bye, especially David.*

ACTS 15:39 | *Their disagreement was so sharp that they separated. Barnabas took John Mark with him and sailed for Cyprus.*

1 THESSALONIANS 2:17 | *Dear brothers and sisters, after we were separated from you for a little while (though our hearts never left you), we tried very hard to come back because of our intense longing to see you again.*

You live in a sinful, fallen world. Therefore, you will sometimes be separated from friends and family for various reasons. Sometimes you are lonely because you have hurt those you care about and they have turned their backs on you. Sometimes your friends stop being your friends for reasons you don't understand. And sometimes you have to say good-bye when a friend moves away. God doesn't want you to be lonely, but in this life he allows people's actions to take their natural course. In each of these circumstances, he promises to help you learn from it, and he promises to never leave you, always supplying you with comfort and strength when you ask (see Deuteronomy 31:8; Philippians 4:19).

How can God help me with my loneliness?

PSALM 23:4 | *Even when I walk through the darkest valley . . . you are close beside me.*

PSALM 139:17 | *How precious are your thoughts about me, O God. They cannot be numbered!*

ISAIAH 54:10 | *The mountains may move and the hills disappear, but even then my faithful love for you will remain.*

Recognize that you are not unlovable or deficient just because you are lonely. You have value because God made you, loves you, and promises to be with you.

1 KINGS 19:4 | *[Elijah] sat down under a solitary broom tree and prayed that he might die.*

Loneliness can cause you to feel sorry for yourself, become discouraged, and fall prey to temptation. Don't give up on God when you are lonely. Be careful not to separate yourself from the One who wants to be with you always.

MATTHEW 11:2-3 | *John the Baptist, who was in prison . . . sent his disciples to ask Jesus, "Are you the Messiah we've been expecting, or should we keep looking for someone else?"*

1 PETER 4:19 | *If you are suffering in a manner that pleases God, keep on doing what is right, and trust your lives to the God who created you, for he will never fail you.*

Sometimes you may feel alone in your stand for Christ. Take comfort in knowing that there are others who are equally committed and that God rewards your bold commitment to him.

ISAIAH 41:10 | *Don't be afraid, for I am with you. Don't be discouraged, for I am your God. I will strengthen you and help you. I will hold you up with my victorious right hand.*

JOHN 14:1 | *Don't let your hearts be troubled. Trust in God, and trust also in me.*

Loneliness can cause you to be afraid. But knowing that God is with you and fighting for you can calm your fears.

ROMANS 8:38-39 | *Nothing can ever separate us from God's love. Neither death nor life, neither angels nor demons, neither our fears for today nor our worries about tomorrow—not even the powers of hell can separate us from God's love. No power in the sky above or in the earth below—indeed, nothing in all creation will ever be able to separate us from the love of God that is revealed in Christ Jesus our Lord.*

God has promised he will always be there for you. Nothing can separate you from him. When your human relationships fail, take comfort in your friendship with God.

Promise from God PSALM 23:4 | *Even when I walk through the darkest valley . . . you are close beside me.*

LOVE

How can I love people, even those I don't like?

JOHN 13:34-35 | *[Jesus said,] "I am giving you a new commandment: Love each other. Just as I have loved you, you should love each other. Your love for one another will prove to the world that you are my disciples."*

1 PETER 4:8 | *Most important of all, continue to show deep love for each other, for love covers a multitude of sins.*

1 JOHN 2:9 | *If anyone claims, "I am living in the light," but hates a Christian brother or sister, that person is still living in darkness.*

1 JOHN 4:12 | *If we love each other, God lives in us, and his love is brought to full expression in us.*

Being a Christian comes with certain expectations, and one of them is that you will love others. Loving others is one of the proofs that you belong to Christ.

GALATIANS 6:8-10 | *Those who live to please the Spirit will harvest everlasting life from the Spirit. So let's not get tired of doing what is good. At just the right time we will reap a harvest of blessing if we don't give up. Therefore, whenever we have the opportunity, we should do good to everyone—especially to those in the family of faith.*

The Holy Spirit awakens love for others. You can ask God to make you willing to love others, even those who are difficult to love, and God will hear your prayers.

Does God really love me? How can I know?

JOHN 3:16 | *God loved the world so much that he gave his one and only Son, so that everyone who believes in him will not perish but have eternal life.*

1 JOHN 4:9-10 | *God showed how much he loved us by sending his one and only Son into the world so that we might have eternal life through him. This is real love—not that we loved God, but that he loved us and sent his Son as a sacrifice to take away our sins.*

God loves you so much he sent his Son, Jesus, to earth to die for you. Jesus took the punishment you deserve for your sins. His forgiveness is so complete it is as though you never sinned at all. His love for you can never be changed or broken.

ROMANS 5:5 | *We know how dearly God loves us, because he has given us the Holy Spirit to fill our hearts with his love.*

The Holy Spirit's presence in your heart shows God's love for you because he is always with you, always helping you, always showing you the best way to live.

How should I show my love to God?

JOHN 14:21 | *Those who accept my commandments and obey them are the ones who love me.*

Love God by obeying him and respecting his commandments.

PSALM 122:1 | *I was glad when they said to me, "Let us go to the house of the LORD."*

Love God by worshiping him and praising him for his love for you.

HEBREWS 6:10 | *[God] will not forget how hard you have worked for him and how you have shown your love to him by caring for other believers, as you still do.*

Love God by guiding and helping Jesus' followers and by being an example to others.

MATTHEW 10:42 | *If you give even a cup of cold water to one of the least of my followers, you will surely be rewarded.*

Show love to needy people, whom God loves.

Promise from God ROMANS 8:39 | *No power in the sky above or in the earth below—indeed, nothing in all creation will ever be able to separate us from the love of God that is revealed in Christ Jesus our Lord.*

LUST

What is the difference between lust and love?

2 SAMUEL 13:14 | *Amnon wouldn't listen to [Tamar], and since he was stronger than she was, he raped her.*

Love gives time after time and never takes that which is not offered. Lust takes what it wants regardless of another's needs or desires.

1 CORINTHIANS 13:4-5 | *Love is patient and kind. . . . It does not demand its own way.*

Love is patient and kind. Lust is impatient and rude.

Since lust involves the mind and not actual physical behavior, why is it wrong?

LUKE 11:34 | *Your eye is a lamp that provides light for your body. When your eye is good, your whole body is filled with light. But when it is bad, your body is filled with darkness.*

Every action begins as a thought. Left unchecked, wrong thoughts will eventually result in wrong actions. When lust is allowed to take up residence in your mind, it tends to consume your thoughts and the light of God is pushed aside.

1 KINGS 11:3 | *[Solomon] had 700 wives of royal birth and 300 concubines. And in fact, they did turn his heart away from the LORD.*

Because lust is a sin, dwelling on it or consistently giving in to it (Solomon had one thousand wives and concubines!) will have a negative impact on your behavior and turn your heart from God. Solomon's lust led not only to promiscuity but eventually to a rejection of God.

How can I keep my desires from becoming lustful?

MATTHEW 5:28 | *Anyone who even looks at a woman with lust has already committed adultery with her in his heart.*

You can prevent lust from taking root in your mind by not taking that "second look."

PHILIPPIANS 4:8 | *Fix your thoughts on what is true, and honorable, and right, and pure, and lovely, and admirable. Think about things that are excellent and worthy of praise.*

When you fill your heart and mind with what is pure and good, lust finds no place to dwell.

SONG OF SONGS 7:6 | *Oh, how beautiful you are! How pleasing, my love, how full of delights!*

God created you to experience the joys of sexual intimacy. Song of Songs reminds you that your pleasure is truly fulfilling only when pursued in accordance with God's standards of love, purity, and marriage.

Is it possible to lust for something other than physical pleasure?

EXODUS 20:17 | *You must not covet your neighbor's house.*

JOB 22:24-25 | *If you give up your lust for money and throw your precious gold into the river, the Almighty himself will be your treasure.*

It is possible to lust for many things: Power, wealth, and material things can all become objects of lust.

Promise from God 2 TIMOTHY 2:22 | *Run from anything that stimulates youthful lusts. Instead, pursue righteous living, faithfulness, love, and peace. Enjoy the companionship of those who call on the Lord with pure hearts.*

LYING

Why is it so important to tell the truth?

JOHN 14:6 | *Jesus [said], "I am the way, the truth, and the life. No one can come to the Father except through me."*

EPHESIANS 4:25 | *Stop telling lies. Let us tell our neighbors the truth, for we are all parts of the same body.*

God is truth, so lying is in opposition to God. Truth always speaks what is right and good. Lying always seeks to cover up the truth.

PROVERBS 12:22 | *The LORD detests lying lips, but he delights in those who tell the truth.*

LUKE 16:10 | *If you are dishonest in little things, you won't be honest with greater responsibilities.*

Telling the truth is a litmus test to see if you are trying to model your life after the God of truth. Telling the truth is the only way to have trust in a relationship. And telling the truth is commanded by God.

Is lying ever justified?

PSALM 25:21 | *May integrity and honesty protect me, for I put my hope in you.*

PSALM 119:163 | *I hate and abhor all falsehood, but I love your instructions.*

PROVERBS 12:17 | *An honest witness tells the truth; a false witness tells lies.*

PROVERBS 13:5 | *The godly hate lies; the wicked cause shame and disgrace.*

PROVERBS 20:10 | *False weights and unequal measures—the LORD detests double standards of every kind.*

While it is hard to always tell the truth, God wants your heart to always *want* to tell the truth. God is not pleased when you tell the truth just to benefit yourself.

Promise from God PROVERBS 12:19 | *Truthful words stand the test of time, but lies are soon exposed.*

MATURITY

How can I reach the Christian maturity I desire?

EPHESIANS 3:17 | *Christ will make his home in your hearts as you trust in him. Your roots will grow down into God's love and keep you strong.*

COLOSSIANS 2:7 | *Let your roots grow down into him, and let your lives be built on him. Then your faith will grow strong in the truth you were taught, and you will overflow with thankfulness.*

Reading the Bible and praying to God are the first and most important steps toward Christian maturity. Because God is the source of all wisdom, he is the ultimate example of maturity. You should model your life after Jesus, who was the embodiment of God and godly wisdom.

1 CORINTHIANS 3:1-2 | *[Paul said,] "Dear brothers and sisters, when I was with you I couldn't talk to you as I would to spiritual people. I had to talk as though you belonged to this world*

or as though you were infants in the Christian life. I had to feed you with milk, not with solid food, because you weren't ready for anything stronger."

1 CORINTHIANS 13:11 | *When I was a child, I spoke and thought and reasoned as a child. But when I grew up, I put away childish things.*

HEBREWS 6:1 | *Let us stop going over the basic teachings about Christ again and again. Let us go on instead and become mature in our understanding.*

Spiritual growth is like physical growth—you start small and immature and then you grow up, one day at a time, gaining wisdom and maturity.

JOSHUA 1:1-2 | *After the death of Moses the LORD's servant, the LORD spoke to Joshua son of Nun, Moses' assistant. He said, "Moses my servant is dead. Therefore, the time has come for you to lead these people."*

Good spiritual mentors can help you grow and mature in your faith, as well as in everyday life. Look for people who are several stages ahead of you in life, who have weathered many experiences, and who exemplify godliness. Ask them to help you learn how to become a mature Christian and a mature person.

1 CORINTHIANS 9:25 | *All athletes are disciplined in their training. They do it to win a prize that will fade away, but we do it for an eternal prize.*

To reach spiritual maturity, you must discipline yourself like an athlete does. Athletes excel as they exercise and push the boundaries of their physical capabilities. When you give the same emphasis to spiritual discipline, you will experience a deepening faith and a maturity in the way you approach life.

What can keep me from maturing? What should I avoid?

ISAIAH 59:2 | *It's your sins that have cut you off from God.*

2 TIMOTHY 2:4 | *Soldiers don't get tied up in the affairs of civilian life, for then they cannot please the officer who enlisted them.*

When you allow yourself to get sidetracked by temptation, you lose sight of what is truly important. Just as a child acts upon immediate desires, temptation causes you to sin, which keeps you spiritually immature in some way. True maturity is recognizing and resisting the temptations that would slow down your journey toward the goals God has set for you.

Promise from God PHILIPPIANS 4:13 | *I can do everything through Christ, who gives me strength.*

MEANING

What brings meaning to my life? What will make my life count?

GENESIS 1:26 | *God said, "Let us make human beings in our image, to be like us. They will reign over the fish in the sea, the birds in the sky, the livestock, all the wild animals on the earth, and the small animals that scurry along the ground."*

ROMANS 11:36 | *Everything comes from [the Lord] and exists by his power and is intended for his glory. All glory to him forever!*

God, as your Creator, gives you value. You are made in his image, and his very breath gives you life.

EZEKIEL 29:21 | *They will know that I am the LORD.*

You are created to know God and enjoy fellowship with him. What could be more meaningful than a relationship with God, your Creator?

PSALM 8:3-8 | *When I look at the night sky and see the work of your fingers—the moon and the stars you set in place—what are mere mortals that you should think about them, human beings that you should care for them? Yet you made them only a little lower than God and crowned them with glory and honor. You gave them charge of everything you made, putting all things under their authority—the flocks and the herds and all the wild animals, the birds in the sky, the fish in the sea, and everything that swims the ocean currents.*

God has given humans first place in Creation and the great responsibility of managing and caring for Creation. This is a meaningful purpose and a high honor!

MATTHEW 4:19 | *Jesus called out . . . "Come, follow me, and I will show you how to fish for people!"*

2 CORINTHIANS 5:18 | *God . . . brought us back to himself through Christ. And God has given us this task of reconciling people to him.*

You are called to participate in God's work in the world and make an eternal impact on others for him.

JOHN 11:25-26 | *Jesus [said], "I am the resurrection and the life. Anyone who believes in me will live, even after dying. Everyone who lives in me and believes in me will never ever die."*

The fact that death is not the end for Jesus' followers invests your life with eternal significance. Knowing there is life after death gives you true perspective on what you do here and now.

PSALM 16:11 | *You will show me the way of life, granting me the joy of your presence and the pleasures of living with you forever.*

PHILIPPIANS 1:9-10 | *I pray that your love will overflow more and more, and that you will keep on growing in knowledge and understanding. For I want you to understand what really matters, so that you may live pure and blameless lives until the day of Christ's return.*

A personal, growing relationship with Jesus Christ today and for eternity gives life meaning. He created you for a purpose, and the better you know him, the clearer his purposes for you will become.

Promise from God PSALM 119:37 | *Turn my eyes from worthless things, and give me life through your word.*

MIRACLES

What are miracles?

ISAIAH 41:19-20 | *I will plant trees in the barren desert—cedar, acacia, myrtle, olive, cypress, fir, and pine. I am doing this so all who see this miracle will understand what it means—that it is the LORD who has done this, the Holy One of Israel who created it.*

HEBREWS 2:4 | *God confirmed the message by giving signs and wonders and various miracles and gifts of the Holy Spirit whenever he chose.*

Miracles are supernatural events. God's miracles are visible signs of his power, authority, presence, and love for his people. They are always about his Kingdom work; they help you know him, encourage you to keep going, rescue you, and help you see his hand in your life.

EXODUS 7:10-12 | *Aaron threw down his staff before Pharaoh and his officials, and it became a serpent! Then Pharaoh called in his own wise men and sorcerers, and these Egyptian magicians did the same thing with their magic. They threw down their staffs, which also became serpents! But then Aaron's staff swallowed up their staffs.*

2 THESSALONIANS 2:9 | *[The man of lawlessness] will come to do the work of Satan with counterfeit power and signs and miracles.*

It is important to note that not all miracles are from God. Satan and his demons have the ability to perform miracles, although they do not have the same power that God has. You can tell when miracles are not from God because the people who perform them will do so only to destroy, to promote themselves or their own interests, or to lead people away from God.

How does God use miracles?

EXODUS 10:1 | *The LORD said to Moses, "Return to Pharaoh and make your demands again. I have made him and his officials stubborn so I can display my miraculous signs among them."*

Sometimes God uses miracles to demonstrate his power.

JOHN 4:50-53 | *Jesus told [the official], "Go back home. Your son will live!" And the man believed what Jesus said and started home. While the man was on his way, some of his servants met him with the news that his son was alive and well. He asked them when the boy had begun to get better, and they replied, "Yesterday afternoon at one o'clock his fever suddenly disappeared!" Then the father realized that that was the very time Jesus had told him, "Your son will live." And he and his entire household believed in Jesus.*

Sometimes God uses miracles to help you believe in him.

MATTHEW 8:3 | *Jesus reached out and touched [the leper]. "I am willing," he said. "Be healed!" And instantly the leprosy disappeared.*

MATTHEW 14:14 | *Jesus saw the huge crowd as he stepped from the boat, and he had compassion on them and healed their sick.*

Sometimes God uses miracles to show his love and his compassion for you.

2 KINGS 17:36 | *Worship only the LORD, who brought you out of Egypt with great strength and a powerful arm. Bow down to him alone, and offer sacrifices only to him.*

DANIEL 6:27 | *[God] rescues and saves his people; he performs miraculous signs and wonders in the heavens and on earth. He has rescued Daniel from the power of the lions.*

MICAH 7:15 | *"Yes," says the LORD, "I will do mighty miracles for you."*

Sometimes God uses miracles to rescue you.

How should I respond when God performs miracles in my life?

LUKE 19:37 | *All of [Jesus'] followers began to shout and sing as they walked along, praising God for all the wonderful miracles they had seen.*

You should offer praise and thanksgiving to him.

PSALM 9:1 | *I will praise you, LORD, with all my heart; I will tell of all the marvelous things you have done.*

You can best show your gratitude to God by telling others what God has done for you and giving him all the credit.

What keeps me from seeing more miracles in my life?

EXODUS 8:17-19 | *Moses and Aaron did just as the LORD had commanded them. When Aaron raised his hand and struck the ground with his staff, gnats infested the entire land, covering the Egyptians and their animals. . . . Pharaoh's magicians tried to do the same thing with their secret arts, but this time they failed. And the gnats covered everyone, people and animals alike. "This is the finger of God!" the magicians exclaimed to Pharaoh. But Pharaoh's heart remained hard. He wouldn't listen to them, just as the LORD had predicted.*

You won't see a miracle if you are too stubborn to believe that a miracle can happen or that God would perform one on your behalf. Even Pharaoh's magicians saw Moses' miracle as an act of God, but Pharaoh was too stubborn to admit it. He convinced himself this couldn't be from the hand of God. When you get rid of pride and stubbornness, you will be surprised to see how much God is doing in your life—things that you never noticed before.

PSALM 106:2 | *Who can list the glorious miracles of the LORD? Who can ever praise him enough?*

Maybe you think a miracle is always a dramatic event such as a dead person coming back to life. But miracles are happening all around you, maybe not as dramatic as the parting of the Red Sea, but no less powerful. The birth of a baby, the healing of an illness, the rebirth of the earth in spring, the gift of salvation by faith alone, a work of love and forgiveness that changes someone, the excitement of hearing the specific call of God in your life are just a few. If you think you've never seen any miracles, look closer. They are happening all around you.

Promise from God LUKE 1:37 | *Nothing is impossible with God.*

MISTAKES

What causes mistakes?

EXODUS 32:1 | *When the people saw how long it was taking Moses to come back down the mountain, they gathered around Aaron. "Come on," they said, "make us some gods who can lead us. We don't know what happened to this fellow Moses, who brought us here from the land of Egypt."*

JOSHUA 8:14 | *When the king of Ai saw the Israelites across the valley, he and all his army hurried out early in the morning and attacked the Israelites at a place overlooking the Jordan Valley. But he didn't realize there was an ambush behind the town.*

PROVERBS 19:2-3 | *Enthusiasm without knowledge is no good; haste makes mistakes. People ruin their lives by their own foolishness and then are angry at the LORD.*

Impatience can lead to poor life choices. When you hurry to act without first checking your assumptions, you can make very serious mistakes.

GENESIS 13:10-13 | *Lot took a long look at the fertile plains of the Jordan Valley. . . . The whole area was well watered everywhere, like the garden of the LORD. . . . Lot chose for himself the whole Jordan Valley to the east of them. . . . So Abram settled in the land of Canaan, and Lot moved his tents to a place near Sodom and settled among the cities of the plain. But the people of this area were extremely wicked and constantly sinned against the LORD.*

1 SAMUEL 13:11-13 | *Samuel said, "What is this you have done?" Saul replied, "I saw my men scattering . . . so I felt compelled to offer the burnt offering myself before you came." "How foolish!" Samuel exclaimed. "You have not kept the command the LORD your God gave you."*

Sometimes your mistakes are created by the selfish pursuit of your own agenda. When your choices are guided primarily by selfish ambition or a desire for physical fulfillment, you are more likely to make a mistake.

1 KINGS 12:3-4, 6, 8-11 | *Jeroboam and the whole assembly of Israel went to speak with Rehoboam. "Your father was a hard master,"*

they said. "*Lighten the harsh labor demands and heavy taxes that your father imposed on us. Then we will be your loyal subjects.*" . . . *Then King Rehoboam discussed the matter with the older men who had counseled his father, Solomon. . . . But Rehoboam rejected the advice of the older men and instead asked the opinion of the young men who had grown up with him and were now his advisers. "What is your advice?" he asked them. . . . The young men replied, "This is what you should tell those complainers who want a lighter burden: '. . . Yes, my father laid heavy burdens on you, but I'm going to make them even heavier! My father beat you with whips, but I will beat you with scorpions!'*"

PROVERBS 12:15 | *Fools think their own way is right, but the wise listen to others.*

Rejecting the advice of wise counselors can lead to mistakes.

When I make a big mistake, how do I move on?

2 SAMUEL 12:13 | *David confessed to Nathan, "I have sinned against the LORD." Nathan replied, "Yes, but the LORD has forgiven you."*

1 JOHN 1:10 | *If we claim we have not sinned, we are calling God a liar and showing that his word has no place in our hearts.*

Begin by admitting your mistakes and sins so you are open to forgiveness and restoration.

1 JOHN 1:9 | *If we confess our sins to him, he is faithful and just to forgive us.*

Receive God's forgiveness. He wants to give it as much as you need to receive it.

JAMES 5:16 | *Confess your sins to each other and pray for each other.*

Offer forgiveness to others, ask for theirs when needed, and receive it when it's extended.

JEREMIAH 8:4-6 | *This is what the LORD says: "When people fall down, don't they get up again? When they discover they're on the wrong road, don't they turn back? Then why do these people stay on their self-destructive path? Why do the people of Jerusalem refuse to turn back? . . . Is anyone sorry for doing wrong? Does anyone say, 'What a terrible thing I have done'?"*

1 CORINTHIANS 10:1, 11 | *I don't want you to forget, dear brothers and sisters, about our ancestors in the wilderness long ago. . . . These things happened to them as examples for us. They were written down to warn us.*

Learn from your mistakes. If you don't learn from them, you will be lulled into a false sense of security. Learning from your past mistakes prepares you to not repeat them in the future.

Promise from God PHILIPPIANS 3:13-14 | *No, dear brothers and sisters, I have not achieved it, but I focus on this one thing: Forgetting the past and looking forward to what lies ahead, I press on to reach the end of the race and receive the heavenly prize for which God, through Christ Jesus, is calling us.*

MODESTY

What is godly modesty?

1 TIMOTHY 2:9 | *I want women to be modest in their appearance. They should wear decent and appropriate clothing and not draw attention to themselves by the way they fix their hair or by wearing gold or pearls or expensive clothes.*

1 PETER 2:12 | *Be careful to live properly among your unbelieving neighbors. Then even if they accuse you of doing wrong, they will see your honorable behavior, and they will give honor to God when he judges the world.*

Godly modesty is maintaining a standard of appropriateness that cannot be criticized and keeps you from being a stumbling block to others. It is keeping your appearance and behavior in harmony with faith, love, and holiness. Modesty frees you from focusing excessive time and attention on yourself and worrying about how you appear to others.

How can I be modest in my appearance?

1 CORINTHIANS 6:19 | *Don't you realize that your body is the temple of the Holy Spirit, who lives in you and was given to you by God? You do not belong to yourself.*

1 PETER 3:3-4 | *Don't be concerned about the outward beauty of fancy hairstyles, expensive jewelry, or beautiful clothes. You should clothe yourselves instead with the beauty that comes from within, the unfading beauty of a gentle and quiet spirit, which is so precious to God.*

By focusing on inward beauty, for that kind of beauty remains strong and youthful long after your body turns old and frail.

How should I show modesty in my behavior?

ROMANS 13:13 | *Because we belong to the day, we must live decent lives for all to see. Don't participate in the darkness of wild parties and drunkenness, or in sexual promiscuity and immoral living, or in quarreling and jealousy.*

EPHESIANS 5:8 | *Once you were full of darkness, but now you have light from the Lord. So live as people of light!*

TITUS 2:12 | *We are instructed to turn from godless living and sinful pleasures. We should live in this evil world with wisdom, righteousness, and devotion to God.*

You can show modesty by avoiding wrong and indecent behavior and by serving others with grace and kindness.

Does being modest mean I shouldn't try to look nice?

ECCLESIASTES 9:7-8 | *Go ahead. Eat your food with joy, and drink your wine with a happy heart, for God approves of this! Wear fine clothes, with a splash of cologne!*

1 CORINTHIANS 6:19-20 | *Don't you realize that your body is the temple of the Holy Spirit, who lives in you and was given to you by God? You do not belong to yourself, for God bought you with a high price. So you must honor God with your body.*

COLOSSIANS 3:17 | *Whatever you do or say, do it as a representative of the Lord Jesus, giving thanks through him to God the Father.*

You should not be obsessed with your physical appearance, but neither should you ignore it. How you present yourself is, in part, a reflection of who you are and plays a role in your ability to interact with others. Your body is the house in which the Holy Spirit dwells, so you should keep up the place in which he lives. The more you keep yourself fit, the more energy you will have to serve him. Keeping your body clean and pleasant looking provides more opportunities to become involved in others' lives and to influence them with the good news of Jesus. However, dressing in a provocative way that tempts someone of the opposite sex or distracts others from seeing Jesus in you is immodest and inappropriate.

Can I show modesty and still have fun?

NEHEMIAH 8:10 | *Go and celebrate with a feast . . . and share gifts of food with people who have nothing prepared. This is a sacred day. . . . Don't be . . . sad, for the joy of the LORD is your strength!*

PROVERBS 13:9 | *The life of the godly is full of light and joy.*

MATTHEW 25:21 | *You have been faithful in handling this small amount. . . . Let's celebrate together!*

Modesty is not about a lack of emotion, fun, or celebration. Joy, celebration, and godly fun are important parts of Christian faith because they lift your spirits and help you see the beauty and meaning in life. However, even in celebration, your appearance and conduct should not be provocative or inappropriate.

Promise from God 1 PETER 2:12 | *Be careful to live properly among your unbelieving neighbors. Then even if they accuse you of doing wrong, they will see your honorable behavior, and they will give honor to God when he judges the world.*

MONEY

What is a proper perspective of money?

MATTHEW 6:21 | *Wherever your treasure is, there the desires of your heart will also be.*

The Bible mentions many wealthy people who loved God (Abraham, David, Joseph of Arimathea, Lydia), while saying nothing negative about the amount of wealth they owned. Scripture doesn't focus on how much money you can or cannot have, but rather on what you do with it. Jesus made one thing clear: Wherever your money goes, your heart will follow after it. So work hard and succeed without guilt, but make sure to work just as hard at finding ways to please God with your money.

PSALM 23:1 | *The LORD is my shepherd; I have all that I need.*

ECCLESIASTES 5:10 | *Those who love money will never have enough. How meaningless to think that wealth brings true happiness!*

Money can cultivate a dangerous craving—the more you have, the more you want. It is a vicious cycle that never has a satisfactory conclusion. Keep reminding yourself that God must be first in your life and that money cannot satisfy your deepest needs.

MATTHEW 6:24 | *No one can serve two masters. . . . You cannot serve both God and money.*

LUKE 18:22-23 | *[Jesus said,] "Sell all your possessions and give the money to the poor, and you will have treasure in heaven. Then come, follow me." But when the man heard this he became very sad, for he was very rich.*

The love of money can get your priorities out of line. The more you have, the more time you must spend to manage it and thus the more important it becomes to you. This doesn't always happen just because you have an abundance of money, but it does tend to happen if you don't watch for it and protect against it.

1 TIMOTHY 6:10 | *The love of money is the root of all kinds of evil. And some people, craving money, have wandered from the true faith and pierced themselves with many sorrows.*

HEBREWS 13:5 | *Don't love money; be satisfied with what you have.*

Money is not the root of all evil; the love of it is!

PROVERBS 19:1 | *Better to be poor and honest than to be dishonest and a fool.*

MARK 8:36 | *What do you benefit if you gain the whole world but lose your own soul?*

No amount of money is worth having if it was gained deceptively or dishonestly. Taking advantage of others to make money is stealing. Those who do this lose far more than they could ever gain.

MARK 12:42-44 | *A poor widow came and dropped in two small coins. Jesus . . . said, "I tell you the truth, this poor widow has given more than all the others who are making contributions. For they gave a tiny part of their surplus, but she, poor as she is, has given everything she had to live on."*

1 JOHN 3:17 | *If someone has enough money to live well and sees a brother or sister in need but shows no compassion—how can God's love be in that person?*

Consistent and generous giving is one of the most effective ways to keep you from being greedy with your money. When your giving meets needs in the lives of others, you will find much deeper satisfaction than if you had spent the money on yourself—or hoarded it.

PROVERBS 3:9-10 | *Honor the LORD with your wealth and with the best part of everything you produce. Then he will fill your barns with grain.*

MALACHI 3:10 | *"Bring all the tithes into the storehouse so there will be enough food in my Temple. If you do," says the LORD of Heaven's Armies, "I will open the windows of heaven for you. I will pour out a blessing so great you won't have enough room to take it in! Try it! Put me to the test!"*

Instead of viewing money as yours, to use as you wish, see it as God's, to use as he wishes. Giving back to God the first part of everything you receive will help you maintain this perspective.

Promise from God MATTHEW 6:31-33 | *Don't worry about these things, saying, "What will we eat? What will we drink? What will we wear?" These things dominate the thoughts of unbelievers, but your heavenly Father already knows all your needs. Seek the Kingdom of God above all else, and live righteously, and he will give you everything you need.*

MOTIVES

Does God care about my motives?

1 CHRONICLES 29:17 | *I know, my God, that you examine our hearts and rejoice when you find integrity there. You know I have done all this with good motives, and I have watched your people offer their gifts willingly and joyously.*

PROVERBS 20:27 | *The LORD's light penetrates the human spirit, exposing every hidden motive.*

PROVERBS 21:27 | *The sacrifice of an evil person is detestable, especially when it is offered with wrong motives.*

Your motives are very important to God—the condition of your heart is essential to the condition of your relationship with him.

1 SAMUEL 16:7 | *The LORD said to Samuel, "Don't judge by his appearance or height. . . . The LORD doesn't see things the way you see them. People judge by outward appearance, but the LORD looks at the heart."*

God is more concerned about your motives than with your outward appearance or your actions, because your motives reveal what is in your heart.

JAMES 4:3 | *Even when you ask, you don't get it because your motives are all wrong—you want only what will give you pleasure.*

Wrong motives can hinder your prayers when selfishness rules your requests.

How can I have motives that please God?

PSALM 19:14 | *May the words of my mouth and the meditation of my heart be pleasing to you, O LORD, my rock and my redeemer.*

Ask God to change the way you think by changing your heart.

1 CORINTHIANS 4:4 | *My conscience is clear, but that doesn't prove I'm right. It is the Lord himself who will examine me and decide.*

Remember that God alone knows your heart. Ask him to reveal to you any area in which your motives are less than pure.

1 CHRONICLES 28:9 | *Learn to know . . . God . . . intimately. Worship and serve him with your whole heart and a willing mind. For the LORD sees every heart and knows every plan and thought.*

Your attitude toward God is a good indicator of your motives toward others. If you are halfhearted in the way you approach your relationship with God, chances are your motives and actions toward others may also be halfhearted.

PSALM 26:2 | *Put me on trial, LORD, and cross-examine me. Test my motives and my heart.*

PROVERBS 17:3 | *Fire tests the purity of silver and gold, but the LORD tests the heart.*

Welcome it when God tests your motives. This gives you an opportunity to grow.

PROVERBS 21:2 | *People may be right in their own eyes, but the LORD examines their heart.*

Before you do something, remember that God is as interested in your motives as he is in your actions.

Promise from God EZEKIEL 36:26 | *[The Lord said,] "I will give you a new heart, and I will put a new spirit in you. I will take out your stony, stubborn heart and give you a tender, responsive heart."*

MUSIC

Does God like music?

2 CHRONICLES 5:13-14 | *The trumpeters and singers performed together in unison to praise and give thanks to the LORD. Accompanied by trumpets, cymbals, and other instruments, they raised their voices and praised the LORD with these words: "He is good! His faithful love endures forever!" At that moment . . . the glorious presence of the LORD filled the Temple of God.*

God likes music—he came with his powerful presence and entered the Temple during a time of musical worship.

DEUTERONOMY 31:16, 19 | *The LORD said to Moses, . . . "Write down the words of this song, and teach it to the people of Israel. Help them learn it, so it may serve as a witness."*

God wants you to see that, at times, music enables you to express thoughts and emotions that mere words can't. Music can also help you remember people, truths, or events that are important to the church or in carrying on your spiritual heritage. And worship hymns and songs help you memorize Scripture as well as express your love and adoration for God. For all these reasons, music continues to play a significant role in the church today.

PSALM 147:1 | *How good to sing praises to our God! How delightful and how fitting!*

God delights when you use music to praise him.

What role does music have in worship?

1 CHRONICLES 15:16 | *David . . . ordered the Levite leaders to appoint a choir of Levites who were singers and musicians to sing joyful songs to the accompaniment of harps, lyres, and cymbals.*

Throughout Scripture, music was used to worship the Lord. The fact that King David appointed four thousand musicians and singers to serve in the Temple testifies to the importance of music in the Israelites' worship (see 1 Chronicles 23:5). Through the beauty and harmony of music, we testify to the glory and majesty of God and we express our thanks and praise for our Creator and Provider.

Are there types of music that I should stay away from?

PHILIPPIANS 4:8 | *Fix your thoughts on what is true, and honorable, and right, and pure, and lovely, and admirable. Think about things that are excellent and worthy of praise.*

Christians should protect their minds from things that are not pure. You should avoid music and lyrics that lead you to think about false, dishonorable, shameful, or impure things.

Promise from God ISAIAH 51:11 | *Those who have been ransomed by the LORD will return. They will enter Jerusalem singing, crowned with everlasting joy. Sorrow and mourning will disappear, and they will be filled with joy and gladness.*

OBEDIENCE

How important is obedience to God?

DEUTERONOMY 6:18, 24-25 | *Do what is right and good in the LORD's sight, so all will go well with you. . . . The LORD our God commanded us to obey all these decrees and to fear him so he can continue to bless us and preserve our lives, as he has done to this day. For we will be counted as righteous when we obey all the commands the LORD our God has given us.*

JOHN 14:15 | *[Jesus said,] "If you love me, obey my commandments."*

1 JOHN 3:24 | *Those who obey God's commandments remain in fellowship with him, and he with them. And we know he lives in us because the Spirit he gave us lives in us.*

God's commandments are not burdensome obligations but pathways to joyful, meaningful, satisfying lives. And obeying God is the only way to stay in fellowship with him. God's call for your obedience is based on his own commitment to your well-being. Since God is the Creator of life, he knows how life is supposed to work. Obedience demonstrates your willingness to follow through on what he says, your trust that God's way is best for you, and your desire to have a close relationship with him.

In what ways does God want me to obey him?

GENESIS 6:22 | *Noah did everything exactly as God had commanded him.*

DEUTERONOMY 5:32 | *You must be careful to obey all the commands of the LORD your God, following his instructions in every detail.*

God wants you to do everything he asks of you. True obedience is about following every detail of his commands to the best of your ability.

1 SAMUEL 15:22 | *What is more pleasing to the LORD: your burnt offerings and sacrifices or your obedience to his voice? Listen! Obedience is better than sacrifice, and submission is better than offering the fat of rams.*

Obedience to God involves listening to what he says. Only when you truly listen will you know how to fully obey him.

EXODUS 12:28 | *The people of Israel did just as the LORD had commanded through Moses and Aaron.*

ACTS 5:29 | *Peter and the apostles [said], "We must obey God rather than any human authority."*

ROMANS 13:1 | *Everyone must submit to governing authorities. For all authority comes from God, and those in positions of authority have been placed there by God.*

HEBREWS 13:17 | *Obey your spiritual leaders, and do what they say.*

God also commands you to obey your leaders, unless what they ask contradicts God's Word.

Does obedience to God get me into heaven?

GALATIANS 2:16 | *We know that a person is made right with God by faith in Jesus Christ, not by obeying the law. . . . For no one will ever be made right with God by obeying the law.*

Obedience to religious laws or rules is not what saves you for eternity. But when you believe in Jesus and decide to follow him, you are increasingly motivated to obey God out of love for him.

HEBREWS 11:8 | *It was by faith that Abraham obeyed.*

Obedience is motivated by faith, but obedience itself is not the way to heaven; only faith in Jesus Christ as Savior will get you to heaven. Obedience is the result of faith, not the pathway to faith.

How will the Lord help me obey him?

PHILIPPIANS 2:12-13 | *Work hard to show the results of your salvation, obeying God with deep reverence and fear. For God is working in you, giving you the desire and the power to do what pleases him.*

When God requires you to do something, he enables you to do it. Not only does God guide you into the ways that are best for you, but he also gives you the power to live according to those ways.

Promise from God JAMES 1:25 | *If you look carefully into the perfect law that sets you free, and if you do what it says and don't forget what you heard, then God will bless you for doing it.*

OPPORTUNITIES

How do I make the most of opportunities?

JOHN 9:4 | *We must quickly carry out the tasks assigned us by the one who sent us. The night is coming, and then no one can work.*

EPHESIANS 5:16 | *Make the most of every opportunity in these evil days.*

When you see an opportunity to do good, jump at it. The longer you think about it, the less likely you are to act. Even when you are experiencing personal hardship, reach out to others—helping others can be therapeutic.

JEREMIAH 13:16 | *Give glory to the LORD your God before it is too late. Acknowledge him before he brings darkness upon you, causing you to stumble and fall on the darkening mountains.*

Now is the time to respond to God's call and get to know him and his purpose for you. You never know when it will be too late.

1 CORINTHIANS 16:8-9 | *[Paul said,] "I will be staying here at Ephesus until the Festival of Pentecost. There is a wide-open door for a great work here, although many oppose me."*

Be willing to be flexible and to change your plans in order to take advantage of an opportunity.

ACTS 11:19-21 | *The believers who had been scattered during the persecution after Stephen's death traveled as far as Phoenicia, Cyprus, and Antioch of Syria. They preached the word of God, but only to Jews. However, some of the believers who went to Antioch from Cyprus and Cyrene began preaching to the Gentiles about the Lord Jesus. The power of the Lord was with them, and a large number of these Gentiles believed and turned to the Lord.*

Take every opportunity to proclaim the good news of Christ's salvation.

How can I prepare for opportunities before they come?

MATTHEW 9:37-38 | *[Jesus] said to his disciples, "The harvest is great, but the workers are few. So pray to the Lord who is in charge of the harvest."*

Pray that God will prepare you to respond to opportunities as they become available.

JOHN 12:35 | *Jesus [said], "My light will shine for you just a little longer. Walk in the light while you can, so the darkness will not overtake you."*

To walk in the light means to stay as close to Jesus as you can through prayer, Bible study, and fellowship with other Christians. Walking in Christ's light will help you more clearly see the opportunities he sends you.

ACTS 8:30-31, 35 | *Philip ran over and heard the man reading from the prophet Isaiah. Philip asked, "Do you understand what you are reading?" The man replied, "How can I, unless someone instructs me?" . . . So beginning with this same Scripture, Philip told him the Good News about Jesus.*

Always be on the lookout for opportunities to be a witness for your faith in word or deed. God will put them in front of you; you need to act on them. And God promises he will make important spiritual moments from them.

Promise from God MATTHEW 25:29 | *To those who use well what they are given, even more will be given, and they will have an abundance. But from those who do nothing, even what little they have will be taken away.*

PARENTS

How should I treat my parents?

EXODUS 20:12 | *Honor your father and mother. Then you will live a long, full life in the land the LORD your God is giving you.*

MARK 7:12-13 | *You let [people] disregard their needy parents. And so you cancel the word of God.*

EPHESIANS 6:1 | *Children, obey your parents because you belong to the Lord, for this is the right thing to do.*

Even if you disagree with your parents, you must still show them honor, respect, and obedience.

Promise from God EPHESIANS 6:3 | *If you honor your father and mother, "things will go well for you, and you will have a long life on the earth."*

PATIENCE

How do I develop more patience?

JAMES 5:7 | *Consider the farmers who patiently wait for the rains in the fall and in the spring. They eagerly look for the valuable harvest to ripen.*

Whether you're waiting for a traffic jam to unsnarl, a friend to return a call, or God to perfect you, you can become more patient by recognizing that growing in patience takes time and there is only so much you can do to speed up the process. A key to understanding God's will is to trust God's timing.

EXODUS 5:22; 6:2 | *Moses went back to the LORD and protested . . . "Why did you send me?" . . . And God said to Moses, "I am Yahweh—'the LORD.'"*

Focusing less on your agenda and more on God's agenda for you will provide a "big picture" perspective and help you be less impatient.

HABAKKUK 2:3 | *If it seems slow in coming, wait patiently, for it will surely take place. It will not be delayed.*

Patience can actually give you an attitude of excited anticipation for each new day. If God is going to do what is best for you, then his plan for you will be accomplished on his schedule, not yours. Keeping that in mind, you can become excited about waiting for him to act, for you awake each day anticipating what good thing he will work in your life that is just right for you at the present time.

GALATIANS 5:22 | *The Holy Spirit produces this kind of fruit in our lives: love, joy, peace, patience . . .*

The more you let the Holy Spirit fill and inspire you, the more patient you will become. All fruit takes time to grow and mature, including the fruit of the Holy Spirit.

ROMANS 8:25 | *If we look forward to something we don't yet have, we must wait patiently and confidently.*

Patience is a by-product of the hope a believer has in God's plans, especially his eternal plans. When your long-range future is totally secure, you can be more patient with today's frustrations.

1 PETER 2:19-20 | *God is pleased with you when you do what you know is right and patiently endure unfair treatment. Of course,*

you get no credit for being patient if you are beaten for doing wrong. But if you suffer for doing good and endure it patiently, God is pleased with you.

God uses life's circumstances to develop your patience. You can't always choose the circumstances that come your way, but you can choose how you will respond to them.

Promise from God PSALM 40:1 | *I waited patiently for the LORD to help me, and he turned to me and heard my cry.*

PEER PRESSURE

Is all peer pressure bad?

JAMES 4:17 | *Remember, it is sin to know what you ought to do and then not do it.*

No, some peer pressure is good. Good peer pressure will always hold you accountable to the things that God calls you to do.

How do I tell the difference between good and bad peer pressure?

MATTHEW 7:20 | *Just as you can identify a tree by its fruit, so you can identify people by their actions.*

Good peer pressure will always encourage you to live a more godly life, while bad peer pressure will always lead you away from godly living.

How do I best handle peer pressure?

PROVERBS 14:7 | *Stay away from fools, for you won't find knowledge on their lips.*

PROVERBS 24:1 | *Don't envy evil people or desire their company.*

PROVERBS 27:17 | *As iron sharpens iron, so a friend sharpens a friend.*

1 CORINTHIANS 15:33 | *Bad company corrupts good character.*

Perhaps the most obvious and most practical way to resist negative peer pressure is to choose wise peers. If you can't resist friends who constantly persuade you to do wrong, you might need to stay away from them until you have the strength to resist their temptations.

MATTHEW 1:24 | *[Joseph] did as the angel of the Lord commanded and took Mary as his wife.*

Joseph provides an excellent example for you. His friends would have advised him to break off the engagement immediately. However, Joseph chose to obey God rather than people.

MATTHEW 14:9 | *The king regretted what he had said; but because of the vow he had made in front of his guests, he issued the necessary orders.*

Never let pride or the risk of embarrassment keep you from making right choices. Keep your motives pure. Protecting your pride and saving yourself from embarrassment are poor motives for your choices.

LUKE 20:21 | *"Teacher," they said, "we know that you speak and teach what is right and are not influenced by what others think. You teach the way of God truthfully."*

It is easier to resist bad influences when you are grounded in God's Word.

Promise from God   1 CORINTHIANS 10:13 | *The temptations in your life are no different from what others experience. And God is faithful. He will not allow the temptation to be more than you can stand. When you are tempted, he will show you a way out so that you can endure.*

PLANNING

Why should I plan ahead?

PROVERBS 13:16 | *Wise people think before they act; fools don't—and even brag about their foolishness.*

PROVERBS 14:8 | *The prudent understand where they are going, but fools deceive themselves.*

PROVERBS 22:3 | *A prudent person foresees danger and takes precautions. The simpleton goes blindly on and suffers the consequences.*

Planning prepares you for life. The lazy person will always be caught off guard by difficult circumstances, but the person who plans ahead will be able to face the difficulties of life with confidence. Planning allows you to be productive, even in difficult times.

PROVERBS 20:4 | *Those too lazy to plow in the right season will have no food at the harvest.*

LUKE 14:28 | *Don't begin until you count the cost. For who would begin construction of a building without first calculating the cost to see if there is enough money to finish it?*

Planning is a necessary part of living.

How do I plan?

EXODUS 25:1, 40 | *The LORD said to Moses . . . "Be sure that you make everything according to the pattern I have shown you here on the mountain."*

EXODUS 26:30 | *Set up this Tabernacle according to the pattern you were shown on the mountain.*

Follow God's revealed will when you make your plans. You can move ahead with your plans as long as you are confident they do not go against God's Word.

GENESIS 11:4, 8 | *[The people] said, "Come, let's build a great city for ourselves with a tower that reaches into the sky. This will make us famous and keep us from being scattered all over the world." . . . [Then] the LORD scattered them all over the world, and they stopped building the city.*

Making plans without consulting God and what he may want is often a recipe for frustration and disaster.

1 CHRONICLES 28:19 | *"Every part of this plan," David told Solomon, "was given to me in writing from the hand of the LORD."*

PROVERBS 3:5-6 | *Trust in the LORD with all your heart; do not depend on your own understanding. Seek his will in all you do, and he will show you which path to take.*

As you submit to God, he will guide you in making many of your plans.

Promises from God PROVERBS 19:21 | *You can make many plans, but the LORD's purpose will prevail.*

EPHESIANS 1:9-10 | *God has now revealed to us his mysterious plan regarding Christ, a plan to fulfill his own good pleasure.*

And this is the plan: At the right time he will bring everything together under the authority of Christ—everything in heaven and on earth.

POVERTY

Does God really care about the poor?

PSALM 35:10 | *LORD, who can compare with you? . . . Who else protects the helpless and poor from those who rob them?*

PSALM 40:17 | *Since I am poor and needy, let the Lord keep me in his thoughts.*

PSALM 102:17 | *[The Lord] will listen to the prayers of the destitute. He will not reject their pleas.*

PSALM 113:6-8 | *[The Lord] stoops to look down on heaven and on earth. He lifts the poor from the dust and the needy from the garbage dump. He sets them among princes, even the princes of his own people!*

God cares deeply for the poor.

What is my responsibility to the poor?

PROVERBS 19:17 | *If you help the poor, you are lending to the LORD—and he will repay you!*

PROVERBS 22:9 | *Blessed are those who are generous, because they feed the poor.*

ISAIAH 58:10 | *Feed the hungry, and help those in trouble. Then your light will shine out from the darkness, and the darkness around you will be as bright as noon.*

MATTHEW 7:12 | *Do to others whatever you would like them to do to you.*

JAMES 2:9 | *If you favor some people over others, you are committing a sin.*

God has compassion for the poor, so if you want to be more and more like God, you must also have compassion for the poor. Compassion that does not reach into your checkbook or onto your "to do" list is philosophical compassion, not godly compassion. Helping the poor is not merely an obligation but also a privilege that brings you great joy and a reward from God himself.

Promise from God 2 CORINTHIANS 8:9 | *You know the generous grace of our Lord Jesus Christ. Though he was rich, yet for your sakes he became poor, so that by his poverty he could make you rich.*

PRAYER

What is prayer?

2 CHRONICLES 7:14 | *[The Lord said,] "If my people who are called by my name will humble themselves and pray and seek my face and turn from their wicked ways, I will hear from heaven."*

PSALM 9:1-2 | *I will praise you, LORD, with all my heart; I will tell of all the marvelous things you have done. I will be filled with joy because of you. I will sing praises to your name, O Most High.*

PSALM 140:6 | *I said to the LORD, "You are my God!" Listen, O LORD, to my cries for mercy!*

Prayer is conversation with God. It is simply talking with God, honestly telling him your thoughts and feelings, praising him, thanking him, confessing sin, and asking for his help and advice. The essence of prayer is humbly entering the very presence of almighty God.

PSALM 38:18 | *I confess my sins; I am deeply sorry for what I have done.*

1 JOHN 1:9 | *If we confess our sins to him, he is faithful and just to forgive us our sins and to cleanse us.*

Prayer often begins with a confession of sin. It is through confession that you demonstrate the humility necessary for open lines of communication with the almighty, holy God.

1 SAMUEL 14:36 | *The priest said, "Let's ask God first."*

2 SAMUEL 5:19 | *David asked the LORD, "Should I go out to fight the Philistines?"*

Prayer is asking God for guidance and waiting for his direction and leading.

MARK 1:35 | *Before daybreak the next morning, Jesus got up and went out to an isolated place to pray.*

Prayer is an expression of an intimate relationship with your heavenly Father, who makes his own love and resources available to you. Just as you enjoy being with people you love, you enjoy spending time with God the more you get to know him and understand just how much he loves you.

1 SAMUEL 3:10 | *The LORD came and called as before, "Samuel! Samuel!" And Samuel replied, "Speak, your servant is listening."*

Good conversation also includes listening, so make time for God to speak to you. When you listen to God, he will make his wisdom known to you.

Does the Bible teach a "right" way to pray?

1 SAMUEL 23:2 | *David asked the LORD, "Should I go . . . ?"*

NEHEMIAH 1:4 | *For days I mourned, fasted, and prayed to the God of heaven.*

PSALM 18:1 | *I love you, LORD; you are my strength.*

PSALM 32:5 | *Finally, I confessed all my sins to you and stopped trying to hide my guilt. I said to myself, "I will confess my rebellion to the LORD." And you forgave me! All my guilt is gone.*

EPHESIANS 6:18 | *Pray in the Spirit at all times and on every occasion. Stay alert and be persistent in your prayers for all believers everywhere.*

Throughout the Bible, effective prayer includes elements of adoration, fasting, confession, petition, and persistence.

MATTHEW 6:9-13 | *[Jesus said,] "Pray like this: Our Father in heaven, may your name be kept holy. May your Kingdom come soon. May your will be done on earth, as it is in heaven. Give us today the food we need, and forgive us our sins, as we have forgiven those who sin against us. And don't let us yield to temptation, but rescue us from the evil one."*

Jesus taught his disciples that prayer is an intimate relationship with the Father that includes a dependency for daily needs, a commitment to obedience, and the forgiveness of sin.

Does God always answer prayer?

PSALM 116:1-2 | *I love the LORD because he hears my voice and my prayer for mercy. Because he bends down to listen, I will pray as long as I have breath!*

1 PETER 3:12 | *The eyes of the Lord watch over those who do right, and his ears are open to their prayers. But the Lord turns his face against those who do evil.*

God listens carefully to every prayer and answers it. His answer may be yes, no, or wait. Any loving parent gives all three of these responses to a child. God's answering yes to every request would spoil you and be dangerous to your well-being. Answering no to every request would be vindictive, stingy, and damaging to your spirit. Answering wait to every prayer would be frustrating. God always answers based on what he knows is best for you.

2 CORINTHIANS 12:8-9 | *Three different times [Paul] begged the Lord to take [the thorn in his flesh] away. Each time [the Lord] said, "My grace is all you need. My power works best in weakness."*

Sometimes, like Paul, you will find that God answers prayer by giving you something better than you asked for.

JOHN 14:14 | *[Jesus said,] "Ask me for anything in my name, and I will do it!"*

Jesus' name is not a magic wand. Praying in Jesus' name means praying according to Jesus' character and purposes. When you pray like this, you are asking for what God already wants to give you.

Promise from God   1 PETER 3:12 | *The eyes of the Lord watch over those who do right, and his ears are open to their prayers.*

PRIORITIES

What should be my highest priority?

MARK 12:29-31 | *Jesus [said], "The most important commandment is this: 'Listen, O Israel! The LORD our God is the one and only LORD. And you must love the LORD your God with all your heart, all your soul, all your mind, and all your strength.' The second is equally important: 'Love your neighbor as yourself.' No other commandment is greater than these."*

Jesus clearly stated the two greatest priorities for every person: Love God and love others—in that order—with all you've got.

How do I set priorities?

PROVERBS 3:5-6 | *Trust in the LORD with all your heart; do not depend on your own understanding. Seek his will in all you do, and he will show you which path to take.*

Not only is putting God first in your life your top priority, but it helps put all your other priorities in order as well.

1 KINGS 3:9 | *Give me an understanding heart so that I can govern your people well and know the difference between right and wrong. For who by himself is able to govern this great people of yours?*

Tenaciously seeking after God's wisdom is the way to discern right priorities.

1 SAMUEL 14:36 | *Saul said, "Let's chase the Philistines all night and plunder them until sunrise. Let's destroy every last one of them." His men replied, "We'll do whatever you think is best." But the priest said, "Let's ask God first."*

Get God's input before setting your priorities.

JOHN 3:16 | *God loved the world so much that he gave his one and only Son, so that everyone who believes in him will not perish but have eternal life.*

There is no higher priority than loving and obeying God, accepting Jesus' gift of salvation. Nothing affects your eternal future so significantly, and nothing will alter your immediate future so significantly.

What is the test that reveals my priorities?

PROVERBS 3:5-6 | *Trust in the LORD with all your heart; do not depend on your own understanding. Seek his will in all you do, and he will show you which path to take.*

LUKE 12:34 | *Wherever your treasure is, there the desires of your heart will also be.*

Priorities are scales on which your love for God is weighed. You focus most on what or whom you love most.

Promise from God PROVERBS 3:6 | *Seek [the Lord's] will in all you do, and he will show you which path to take.*

PROFANITY

Profanity is just words. Why is it such a big deal?

PHILIPPIANS 4:8 | *Fix your thoughts on what is true, and honorable, and right, and pure, and lovely, and admirable. Think about things that are excellent and worthy of praise.*

What you say shows everyone what is in your heart and mind. When foul language comes out of you, it indicates impurity inside you. Your mind and heart should be filled with good, not profane, thoughts.

EXODUS 20:7 | *You must not misuse the name of the LORD your God.*

To use the name of God frivolously is to violate God's standard for holiness and shows a lack of respect and reverence for him. This is important enough that God made it one of the Ten Commandments.

EPHESIANS 5:4 | *Obscene stories, foolish talk, and coarse jokes—these are not for you. Instead, let there be thankfulness to God.*

What kind of an impact could you have on others if you replaced all your negative, unhealthy, and profane words with words of kindness, encouragement, and gratitude?

Promise from God   JAMES 3:2 | *If we could control our tongues, we would be perfect and could also control ourselves in every other way.*

PURPOSE

Does God have a special purpose for me?

PSALM 57:2 | *I cry out to God Most High, to God who will fulfill his purpose for me.*

God has a general purpose and a specific purpose for you. Your general purpose is to let the love of Jesus shine through you to make an impact on others. More specifically, God has given you spiritual gifts (see Romans 12:6-8; 1 Corinthians 12:4-11; 1 Peter 4:10-11) and wants you to use them to make a unique contribution in your sphere of influence. The better you fulfill your general purpose, the clearer your specific purpose will become.

ACTS 20:24 | *My life is worth nothing to me unless I use it for finishing the work assigned me by the Lord Jesus—the work of telling others the Good News about the wonderful grace of God.*

Part of God's purpose for you is to bring his good news of salvation to others who need to know it.

2 TIMOTHY 1:9 | *God saved us and called us to live a holy life. He did this, not because we deserved it, but because that was his plan from before the beginning of time—to show us his grace through Christ Jesus.*

You are called by God to live a holy life and to show the love of Jesus to others by the way you live.

How can I discover God's specific purpose for me and fulfill it?

ROMANS 12:1-2 | *Give your bodies to God because of all he has done for you. Let them be a living and holy sacrifice—the kind he will find acceptable. . . . Don't copy the behavior and customs of this world, but let God transform you into a new person by changing the way you think. Then you will learn to know God's will for you, which is good and pleasing and perfect.*

Discovering God's purpose for you begins with your whole-hearted commitment to God. He promises to make his will known to you as you make yourself available to him.

PHILIPPIANS 1:20 | *[Paul said,] "I fully expect and hope . . . that I will continue to be bold for Christ. . . . And I trust that my life will bring honor to Christ, whether I live or die."*

PHILIPPIANS 3:12 | *[Paul said,] "I don't mean to say that I have already achieved these things or that I have already reached perfection. But I press on to possess that perfection for which Christ Jesus first possessed me."*

Paul's great purpose, whether by life or by death, was to win others to Christ. Your purpose will be something you feel compelled to do regardless of the risks.

ACTS 13:2 | *One day as these men were worshiping the Lord and fasting, the Holy Spirit said, "Dedicate Barnabas and Saul for the special work to which I have called them."*

Worshiping, praying, fasting, and participating in relationships with other believers will help you discern God's purpose for your life.

Promise from God PSALM 57:2 | *I cry out to God Most High, to God who will fulfill his purpose for me.*

QUITTING

How can I keep going when I feel like quitting?

NEHEMIAH 4:1-3 | *Sanballat . . . mocked the Jews, saying . . . , "What does this bunch of poor, feeble Jews think they're doing?" . . . Tobiah the Ammonite, who was standing beside him, remarked, "That stone wall would collapse if even a fox walked along the top of it!"*

Faced with an overwhelming task and ridicule from adversaries, Nehemiah kept his eyes on his goal and on his call (see Nehemiah 4:6–6:16). You can resist quitting when you keep yourself focused on your goals.

ACTS 20:22 | *[Paul said,] "I am bound by the Spirit to go to Jerusalem. I don't know what awaits me."*

Paul faced unimaginable hardship yet never gave up, finishing the work to which God had called him. If you believe the Holy Spirit has called you to do something, let his power and encouragement keep you from quitting when the going gets tough.

2 CORINTHIANS 4:8 | *We are pressed on every side by troubles, but we are not crushed. We are perplexed, but not driven to despair.*

Even in the midst of suffering, believers can find strength from Jesus to endure.

MATTHEW 10:22 | *Everyone who endures to the end will be saved.*

GALATIANS 6:9 | *Let's not get tired of doing what is good. At just the right time we will reap a harvest of blessing if we don't give up.*

2 TIMOTHY 4:7 | *I have fought the good fight, I have finished the race, and I have remained faithful.*

You can avoid discouragement and the desire to quit by keeping your eyes on the goal of finishing well and on the reward of heaven.

Promise from God MATTHEW 10:22 | *All nations will hate you because you are my followers. But everyone who endures to the end will be saved.*

RACISM

What does the Bible say about racism?

JOHN 4:9 | *[The woman] said to Jesus, "You are a Jew, and I am a Samaritan woman. Why are you asking me for a drink?"*

Although Samaritans were hated by the Jews because of their mixed racial heritage, Jesus went out of his way to have a life-changing conversation with a Samaritan woman.

LUKE 10:33-35 | *[Jesus said,] "A despised Samaritan came along . . . [and] soothed his wounds with olive oil and wine and bandaged them. Then he put the man on his own donkey and took him to an inn, where he took care of him. The next day he handed the innkeeper two silver coins, telling him, 'Take care of this man. If his bill runs higher than this, I'll pay you the next time I'm here.'"*

Jesus confounded his listeners by making a despised Samaritan the hero of one of his most famous parables.

COLOSSIANS 3:11 | *It doesn't matter if you are a Jew or a Gentile, circumcised or uncircumcised, barbaric, uncivilized, slave, or free. Christ is all that matters, and he lives in all of us.*

The church of Jesus Christ should be color blind, believing that all people are created equal.

EPHESIANS 2:14 | *Christ himself has brought peace to us. He united Jews and Gentiles into one people when, in his own body on the cross, he broke down the wall of hostility that separated us.*

Christ died to destroy all the barriers of hostility that sin had created between people.

GALATIANS 3:28 | *There is no longer Jew or Gentile, slave or free, male and female. For you are all one in Christ Jesus.*

Regardless of background, sex, or race, the presence of Christ in the lives of believers makes us all one in him.

Promise from God GALATIANS 3:28 | *There is no longer Jew or Gentile, slave or free, male and female. For you are all one in Christ Jesus.*

RECONCILIATION

What does it mean to be reconciled to God?

ROMANS 5:10 | *Since our friendship with God was restored by the death of his Son while we were still his enemies, we will certainly be saved through the life of his Son.*

EPHESIANS 2:13 | *Now you have been united with Christ Jesus. Once you were far away from God, but now you have been brought near to him through the blood of Christ.*

COLOSSIANS 1:20-21 | *Through [Christ] God reconciled everything to himself. He made peace with everything in heaven and on earth by means of Christ's blood on the cross. This includes you who were once far away from God.*

One of the most fundamental truths taught in the Bible is that all people, including you, are born with a sinful nature, and sin separates you from God. If you want a personal relationship with him, you must be reconciled to him, which begins with the recognition that without the work of Jesus Christ on the cross, you cannot approach God. God chose to have his Son, Jesus, take your punishment so you could approach God. Accept God's gift of bridging the gap so you can be reconciled to him and have a relationship with him. This is the greatest gift ever offered—and the only way to be reconciled to God.

Why is reconciliation between people important?

MATTHEW 5:23-24 | *If you are presenting a sacrifice at the altar in the Temple and you suddenly remember that someone has something against you, leave your sacrifice there at the altar. Go and be reconciled to that person. Then come and offer your sacrifice to God.*

Being reconciled with other people is important to God because it demonstrates a humble and forgiving spirit, which is essential to healthy relationships.

MATTHEW 5:25-26 | *When you are on the way to court with your adversary, settle your differences quickly. Otherwise, your accuser may hand you over to the judge, who will hand you over to an officer, and you will be thrown into prison. And if that happens, you surely won't be free again until you have paid the last penny.*

Working for reconciliation with others is important to your own well-being and peace of mind.

MATTHEW 18:15 | *If another believer sins against you, go privately and point out the offense. If the other person listens and confesses it, you have won that person back.*

God wants you to resolve your differences with others because doing so promotes unity.

Promise from God COLOSSIANS 1:20-22 | *God reconciled everything to himself. . . . This includes you who were once far away from God. You were his enemies, separated from him by your evil thoughts and actions. Yet now he has reconciled you to himself through the death of Christ in his physical body. As a result, he has brought you into his own presence, and you are holy and blameless as you stand before him without a single fault.*

REGRETS

How can I deal with regrets in my life?

2 CORINTHIANS 5:17 | *Anyone who belongs to Christ has become a new person. The old life is gone; a new life has begun!*

When you come to faith in Jesus, he forgives your sins— all of them. Your past is forgotten to him, and he gives you a fresh start. You will still have to live with the consequences of your sins because they are not necessarily retracted. But because God forgives you, you can move forward without the tremendous guilt that can accompany regret.

PSALM 31:10 | *I am dying from grief; my years are shortened by sadness. Sin has drained my strength; I am wasting away from within.*

PHILIPPIANS 3:13 | *I focus on this one thing: Forgetting the past and looking forward to what lies ahead.*

Focus on God, who controls the future, not on regrets of the past. God doesn't cause regrets; he washes them away when you ask him to walk with you into the future.

MATTHEW 26:73-75 | *Some of the other bystanders came over to Peter and said, "You must be one of them; we can tell by your Galilean accent." Peter swore, "A curse on me if I'm lying—I don't know the man!" And immediately the rooster crowed. Suddenly, Jesus' words flashed through Peter's mind: "Before the rooster crows, you will deny three times that you even know me." And he went away, weeping bitterly.*

GALATIANS 2:7-9 | *God had given . . . Peter the responsibility of preaching to the Jews. . . . God . . . worked through Peter as the apostle to the Jews. . . . In fact, James, Peter, and John . . . were known as pillars of the church.*

Turn your regrets into resolve. Regrets can be so powerful that they disable you from serving God in the future. If Peter had focused on his regret over denying Jesus, he would never have been able to preach the good news about Jesus so powerfully. Don't let regret paralyze you; instead, let it motivate you to positive action for God in the future.

PSALM 30:11 | *You have turned my mourning into joyful dancing. You have taken away my clothes of mourning and clothed me with joy.*

PSALM 51:12 | *Restore to me the joy of your salvation, and make me willing to obey you.*

Let your regrets draw you closer to God. Don't let them pull you away from God. He wants to take your burdens from you and restore your relationship with him and others. Don't cause the biggest regret of your life—withdrawing from God. No matter what you've done, he welcomes you with loving arms.

ROMANS 8:28 | *God causes everything to work together for the good of those who love God and are called according to his purpose for them.*

Remember that God has the ability to turn bad into good. He can use even the things you regret to accomplish his will.

1 CHRONICLES 21:8 | *David said to God, "I have sinned greatly by taking this census. Please forgive my guilt for doing this foolish thing."*

MATTHEW 18:21-22 | *Peter came to [Jesus] and asked, "Lord, how often should I forgive someone who sins against me? Seven times?" "No, not seven times," Jesus replied, "but seventy times seven!"*

LUKE 15:18 | *I will go home to my father and say, "Father, I have sinned against both heaven and you."*

Sin always brings regret because it damages the relationships most important to you. Whether it is your own sin or the sin of someone against you, sin causes a deep rift in a relationship; now you are facing conflict, separation, loneliness, frustration, anger, and other kinds of emotions. Forgiveness—whether confessing your sin to God and others or granting forgiveness to others—is the only way to give your heart a chance to start over. It doesn't take away past regrets, but it changes your perspective from regret to restoration. It keeps you focused on the healing that can happen in the future rather than on the wounds that you caused (or received) in the past.

Promise from God 2 CORINTHIANS 7:10 | *The kind of sorrow God wants us to experience leads us away from sin and results in salvation. There's no regret for that kind of sorrow.*

REPENTANCE

What is repentance?

MATTHEW 3:2 | *Repent of your sins and turn to God, for the Kingdom of Heaven is near.*

MATTHEW 16:24 | *Jesus said to his disciples, "If any of you wants to be my follower, you must turn from your selfish ways, take up your cross, and follow me."*

Repentance is being sorry for sin and being committed to a new way of life—that of serving God. It means turning from a life that is ruled by your sinful nature and turning to God for a new nature, which is yours when God's Spirit comes to live in you.

PSALM 32:3-5 | *When I refused to confess my sin, my body wasted away, and I groaned all day long. Day and night your hand of discipline was heavy on me. My strength evaporated like water in the summer heat. Finally, I confessed all my sins*

*to you and stopped trying to hide my guilt. I said to myself,
"I will confess my rebellion to the LORD." And you forgave me!
All my guilt is gone.*

1 JOHN 1:9-10 | *If we confess our sins to him, he is faithful and
just to forgive us our sins and to cleanse us from all wickedness.
If we claim we have not sinned, we are calling God a liar and
showing that his word has no place in our hearts.*

One of the first essential steps to repentance is confession,
which means being humbly honest with God and sincerely
sorry for your sins—the ones you know about and the ones
you are unaware of. Confession restores your relationship
with God, and this renews your strength and spirit. When
you repent, God removes your guilt, restores your joy, and
heals your broken soul. A heart that truly longs for change
is necessary in order for repentance to be genuine.

Why is repentance necessary?

ROMANS 3:23 | *Everyone has sinned; we all fall short of God's
glorious standard.*

Repentance is necessary because every person ever born has
sinned against God and betrayed him.

2 CHRONICLES 30:9 | *The LORD your God is gracious and merci-
ful. If you return to him, he will not continue to turn his face
from you.*

JEREMIAH 3:22 | *"My wayward children," says the LORD, "come
back to me, and I will heal your wayward hearts." "Yes, we're
coming," the people reply, "for you are the LORD our God."*

Repentance is necessary for an ongoing relationship with God. Turn away from anything that is preventing you from worshiping and obeying God wholeheartedly.

JEREMIAH 3:12 | *This is what the LORD says: "O Israel, my faithless people, come home to me again, for I am merciful. I will not be angry with you forever."*

1 TIMOTHY 1:16 | *God had mercy on me so that Christ Jesus could use me as a prime example of his great patience with even the worst sinners. Then others will realize that they, too, can believe in him and receive eternal life.*

Repentance is your only hope of receiving God's mercy. Those who refuse to see and admit their own sins can't be forgiven for them, thereby placing themselves outside God's mercy and blessing.

GALATIANS 2:20 | *My old self has been crucified with Christ. It is no longer I who live, but Christ lives in me.*

TITUS 3:5 | *[God] saved us, not because of the righteous things we had done, but because of his mercy. He washed away our sins, giving us a new birth and new life through the Holy Spirit.*

Repentance allows you to receive a new life from God: literally, a life where the very Spirit of God lives within you.

LUKE 24:47 | *There is forgiveness of sins for all who repent.*

Repentance allows you to receive forgiveness of sin. If you are sincere when you come to God and ask him humbly, he will forgive your sin.

Is repentance a onetime event, or do I need to repent each time I sin?

PSALM 51:17 | *The sacrifice you desire is a broken spirit. You will not reject a broken and repentant heart, O God.*

While salvation is a onetime event, God is pleased by broken and contrite hearts that are willing to continually confess and repent of sin.

1 JOHN 1:8-9 | *If we claim we have no sin, we are only fooling ourselves and not living in the truth. But if we confess our sins to him, he is faithful and just to forgive us.*

Confessing and repenting of sin are daily habits of a person walking in fellowship with God.

Promise from God ACTS 2:38 | *Each of you must repent of your sins and turn to God, and be baptized in the name of Jesus Christ for the forgiveness of your sins. Then you will receive the gift of the Holy Spirit.*

RESURRECTION

How can I have confidence that God will someday resurrect me and fit me for heaven?

1 CORINTHIANS 15:12-14 | *Since we preach that Christ rose from the dead, why are some of you saying there will be no resurrection of the dead? For if there is no resurrection of the dead, then Christ has not been raised either. And if Christ has not been raised, then all our preaching is useless, and your faith is useless.*

If Christ had not defeated death, there would be no hope for eternal life. The fact that Christ did come back to life gives you great confidence in God's promise to also raise you from the dead.

What does Jesus' resurrection mean for me?

JOHN 3:16 | *God loved the world so much that he gave his one and only Son, so that everyone who believes in him will not perish but have eternal life.*

1 CORINTHIANS 15:42 | *It is the same way with the resurrection of the dead. Our earthly bodies are planted in the ground when we die, but they will be raised to live forever.*

The power of God that brought Jesus back from the dead will also bring you back to life. Jesus' death was not the end. His resurrection was the beginning of eternal life for all who believe in him.

1 PETER 1:21 | *Through Christ you have come to trust in God. And you have placed your faith and hope in God because he raised Christ from the dead and gave him great glory.*

The Resurrection, the greatest event in history, is the foundation of your hope. Jesus promised that he would rise from the dead, and because he did, you can be assured that all the other promises God makes to you will also come true.

Promise from God JOHN 11:25-26 | *Jesus [said], "I am the resurrection and the life. Anyone who believes in me will live, even after dying. Everyone who lives in me and believes in me will never ever die."*

RIDICULE

How should I respond to ridicule?

2 CHRONICLES 30:6, 10 | *At the king's command, runners were sent throughout Israel and Judah. They carried letters that said: "O people of Israel, return to the LORD.". . . The runners went from town to town. . . . But most of the people just laughed at the runners and made fun of them.*

1 PETER 2:21, 23 | *God called you to do good, even if it means suffering, just as Christ suffered for you. He is your example, and you must follow in his steps. . . . He did not retaliate when he was insulted, nor threaten revenge when he suffered. He left his case in the hands of God, who always judges fairly.*

Ridicule is nothing more than unkind words designed to inflict pain on another person. Responding to hurtful words with hurtful words of your own does not help the situation, nor is it a godly response. It is better either to respond in love or to say nothing at all. Let God take care of those who ridicule you.

NEHEMIAH 4:4 | *I prayed, "Hear us, our God, for we are being mocked. May their scoffing fall back on their own heads, and may they themselves become captives in a foreign land!"*

You should pray, which draws your focus up to God and away from hurtful words and insults. It connects you to God's strength so you can respond with grace.

MATTHEW 5:11-12 | *God blesses you when people mock you and persecute you and lie about you and say all sorts of evil things against you because you are my followers. Be happy about it! Be very glad! For a great reward awaits you in heaven.*

And remember, the ancient prophets were persecuted in the same way.

Draw strength from the knowledge that it is a privilege to be ridiculed for standing up for what you believe in. God promises a great reward in heaven for those who are ridiculed for following him.

Promise from God   1 PETER 4:14 | *Be happy when you are insulted for being a Christian, for then the glorious Spirit of God rests upon you.*

RISK

What kinds of risks should Christians take?

GENESIS 12:1 | *The LORD had said to Abram, "Leave your native country, your relatives, and your father's family, and go to the land that I will show you."*

NUMBERS 14:6-9 | *Two of the men who had explored the land, Joshua son of Nun and Caleb son of Jephunneh . . . said to all the people of Israel, "The land we traveled through and explored is a wonderful land! And if the LORD is pleased with us, he will bring us safely into that land and give it to us. It is a rich land flowing with milk and honey. Do not rebel against the LORD, and don't be afraid of the people of the land. . . . They have no protection, but the LORD is with us! Don't be afraid of them!"*

Be prepared to risk your resources, your reputation, and possibly even your closest relationships to be faithful to God. Joshua and Caleb, unlike the other spies (see Numbers 13:30-33), were willing to risk all because they trusted God's promises more than they feared the human risks. The only thing more risky than trusting God is *not* trusting him!

LUKE 5:4-7 | *[Jesus] said to Simon, "Now go out where it is deeper, and let down your nets to catch some fish." "Master," Simon replied, "we worked hard all last night and didn't catch a thing. But if you say so, I'll let the nets down again." And this time their nets were so full of fish they began to tear! A shout for help brought their partners in the other boat, and soon both boats were filled with fish and on the verge of sinking.*

Some risks you feel the Lord is asking you to take may appear to be foolish or contrary to your experience. But such risks, done in obedience, yield rich rewards.

ACTS 5:41 | *The apostles left the high council rejoicing that God had counted them worthy to suffer disgrace for the name of Jesus.*

You may risk rejection and loss of security, as the apostles did by preaching about Jesus in the face of persecution, but the rewards of loyalty to God are eternal.

EXODUS 3:10-11 | *[God said,] "Now go, for I am sending you to Pharaoh. You must lead my people Israel out of Egypt." But Moses protested to God, "Who am I to appear before Pharaoh? Who am I to lead the people of Israel out of Egypt?"*

LUKE 1:38 | *Mary responded [to the angel], "I am the Lord's servant. May everything you have said about me come true."*

You must take the risk of doing things God's way. When God asks you to follow him, he often doesn't give you all the information about what will happen. When you step out in faith, he gives guidance as you go. Moses risked his life by approaching Pharaoh and leading the Israelites out of captivity. Mary risked her marriage, her reputation, and her future by being willing to be the mother of Jesus. Following God's will is not without risks, but there is no greater reward.

Promise from God   PSALM 37:5 | *Commit everything you do to the LORD. Trust him, and he will help you.*

SALVATION

What does it mean to be saved?

ROMANS 3:24 | *God, with undeserved kindness, declares that we are righteous. He did this through Christ Jesus when he freed us from the penalty for our sins.*

ROMANS 4:7-8 | *Oh, what joy for those whose disobedience is forgiven, whose sins are put out of sight. Yes, what joy for those whose record the LORD has cleared of sin.*

Being saved, spiritually speaking, means your sins no longer count against you and you are spared from an eternal death sentence. Instead, they are forgiven by the grace of God, and you are given the free gift of eternal life. Being saved does not spare you from earthly troubles, but it does save you from eternal punishment.

PSALM 51:9-10 | *Remove the stain of my guilt. Create in me a clean heart, O God.*

PSALM 103:12 | *[The Lord] has removed our sins as far from us as the east is from the west.*

Being saved means the stain of guilt has been washed away and you have been completely forgiven by God. Your sins not only *appear* to be gone, they *are* gone! You are given a clean slate!

JOHN 5:24 | *[Jesus said,] "I tell you the truth, those who listen to my message and believe in God who sent me have eternal life. They will never be condemned for their sins, but they have already passed from death into life."*

JOHN 10:27-29 | *[Jesus said,] "My sheep listen to my voice; I know them, and they follow me. I give them eternal life, and they will never perish. No one can snatch them away from me, for my Father has given them to me, and he is more powerful than anyone else. No one can snatch them from the Father's hand."*

Being saved means you are assured of living forever in heaven. You will live on a new earth where there will no longer be sin, pain, or suffering (see Revelation 21:4). What greater hope could you have?

How can I be saved?

ROMANS 10:13 | *Everyone who calls on the name of the LORD will be saved.*

God's Word promises salvation—a guarantee of an eternal, perfect life in heaven—to those who call on Jesus' name to have their sins forgiven. Call out to him in prayer and tell him that you want him to save you. He promises he will.

JOHN 3:16 | *God loved the world so much that he gave his one and only Son, so that everyone who believes in him will not perish but have eternal life.*

ROMANS 3:22 | *We are made right with God by placing our faith in Jesus Christ. And this is true for everyone who believes, no matter who we are.*

Jesus promises that those who believe in him will be saved. All you have to do is accept what Jesus did for you. God sent Jesus Christ to take your place and to receive the punishment that your sins demanded. When you believe that he died to save you from your sins and rose again to give you eternal life, you are saved.

ROMANS 10:9-10 | *If you confess with your mouth that Jesus is Lord and believe in your heart that God raised him from the dead, you will be saved. For it is by believing in your heart that you are made right with God, and it is by confessing with your mouth that you are saved.*

EPHESIANS 2:8 | *God saved you by his grace when you believed. And you can't take credit for this; it is a gift from God.*

It seems too easy. The greatest gift God could ever offer— life forever in a perfect world—is absolutely free. You just have to accept it by (1) agreeing with God that you have sinned, (2) acknowledging that your sin cuts you off from God, (3) asking Jesus to forgive your sins, and (4) believing that Jesus is Lord over everything and that he is the Son of God. The gift is yours.

Is salvation available to anyone?

HEBREWS 9:27 | *Each person is destined to die once and after that comes judgment.*

REVELATION 20:12 | *I saw the dead, both great and small, standing before God's throne. And the books were opened, including the Book of Life. And the dead were judged according to what they had done.*

Salvation is available to all, but a time will come when it will be too late to receive it.

How can I be sure of my salvation?

ROMANS 10:9 | *If you confess with your mouth that Jesus is Lord and believe in your heart that God raised him from the dead, you will be saved.*

You can be sure of your salvation because God has promised that you are saved if you believe in Jesus Christ as your Savior.

JOHN 1:12 | *To all who believed him and accepted him, he gave the right to become children of God.*

Just as a child cannot be physically "un-born," God's children, those who have believed in Jesus Christ, cannot be spiritually "un-born." Once you have been born again, you are saved forever.

Why is salvation so central to Christianity?

ROMANS 3:23 | *Everyone has sinned; we all fall short of God's glorious standard.*

ROMANS 6:23 | *The wages of sin is death.*

COLOSSIANS 1:22 | *[God] has reconciled you to himself through the death of Christ in his physical body. As a result, he has brought you into his own presence, and you are holy and blameless as you stand before him without a single fault.*

1 THESSALONIANS 3:13 | *May [the Lord] make your hearts strong, blameless, and holy as you stand before God our Father when our Lord Jesus comes again with all his holy people.*

Salvation is necessary because sin against a holy God separates people from him, bringing judgment and spiritual death. An unholy being cannot live in the presence of a holy God.

ACTS 4:12 | *There is salvation in no one else! God has given no other name under heaven by which we must be saved.*

Although it may sound exclusive, the Bible's claim of "one way" to salvation is actually an expression of the grace and kindness of God in letting all people know how to escape eternal judgment. God invites anyone and everyone to come to him.

Promise from God ROMANS 10:9 | *If you confess with your mouth that Jesus is Lord and believe in your heart that God raised him from the dead, you will be saved.*

SATISFACTION

Why do so many people seem so unhappy?

PSALM 63:1, 5 | *O God, you are my God; I earnestly search for you. My soul thirsts for you; my whole body longs for you in this parched and weary land where there is no water. . . . You satisfy me more than the richest feast.*

ECCLESIASTES 1:8 | *No matter how much we see, we are never satisfied. No matter how much we hear, we are not content.*

JOHN 4:14 | *[Jesus said,] "Those who drink the water I give will never be thirsty again. It becomes a fresh, bubbling spring within them, giving them eternal life."*

Too many people try to meet their deepest needs in ways that just don't satisfy. Sometimes when you're hungry, the worst thing you can do is eat the wrong thing. For example, if you haven't eaten in a while and you quickly gobble down three doughnuts, you'll be satisfied for a few minutes—until you start to shake from the sugar rush. The same principle applies when you attempt to satisfy the hungry soul. If you fill it with fun and pleasure and sin, you'll always be craving more but not getting enough of what you really need. Your soul will get the "shakes." Without taking nourishment from God's spiritual food, you will never feel satisfied and you'll wonder what is wrong with your life.

Does God promise to satisfy all my needs?

PSALM 17:15 | *When I awake, I will see you face to face and be satisfied.*

Spiritual need finds satisfaction in intimacy with God. Since he created you for this purpose, the only way you'll be satisfied is to pursue a relationship with him.

PROVERBS 30:8 | *Give me just enough to satisfy my needs.*

God's first task is often to redefine your needs. There is a vast difference between your needs and your wants. Don't confuse the two.

MATTHEW 5:3 | *[Jesus said,] "God blesses those who . . . realize their need for him, for the Kingdom of Heaven is theirs."*

Jesus promised that the heart hungry for righteousness will be satisfied. Be sure you are hungry for the food that truly satisfies.

Promise from God   PSALM 107:9 | *[The Lord] satisfies the thirsty and fills the hungry with good things.*

SELF-CONTROL

Why can't I seem to control certain desires?

ROMANS 7:21-25 | *I have discovered this principle of life—that when I want to do what is right, I inevitably do what is wrong. I love God's law with all my heart. But there is another power within me that is at war with my mind. This power makes me a slave to the sin that is still within me. Oh, what a miserable person I am! Who will free me from this life that is dominated by sin and death? Thank God! The answer is in Jesus Christ our Lord. So you see how it is: In my mind I really want to obey God's law, but because of my sinful nature I am a slave to sin.*

Because you were born with a sinful nature, it will always be a struggle for you to do what is right and to not do what is wrong. Thankfully, God understands your weaknesses and gives you the desire to please him. As you obey God, you will develop more self-control and the battle with your sinful nature will lessen.

ROMANS 12:1 | *Give your bodies to God because of all he has done for you. Let them be a living and holy sacrifice—the kind he will find acceptable. This is truly the way to worship him.*

You must truly want to give up the wrong desires you have.

What are some steps to exercising self-control?

PSALM 119:9 | *How can a young person stay pure? By obeying your word.*

2 TIMOTHY 2:5 | *Athletes cannot win the prize unless they follow the rules.*

To develop self-control, you first need to know God's guidelines for right living as found in the Bible. You need to know what must be controlled before you can keep it under control. Reading God's Word consistently—preferably every day— keeps his guidelines for right living fresh in your mind.

1 TIMOTHY 4:8 | *Physical training is good, but training for godliness is much better, promising benefits in this life and in the life to come.*

Self-control begins with God's work in you, but it requires your effort as well. Just as talented musicians and athletes must develop their talent, strength, and coordination through intentional effort, spiritual fitness must be intentional as well. God promises to reward such effort.

1 CORINTHIANS 10:13 | *The temptations in your life are no different from what others experience. And God is faithful. He will not allow the temptation to be more than you can stand. When you are tempted, he will show you a way out so that you can endure.*

You're not alone in your trials and temptations. Instead of thinking there is no hope for your resisting, call on the Lord to lead you out of temptation. If you ask, God promises to give you what you need in order to resist. And ask trusted friends to keep you accountable.

PROVERBS 13:3 | *Those who control their tongue will have a long life; opening your mouth can ruin everything.*

JAMES 1:26 | *If you claim to be religious but don't control your tongue, you are fooling yourself, and your religion is worthless.*

You exercise self-control by being careful of what you say. How often do you wish you could take back words as soon as they have left your mouth?

ROMANS 8:6 | *Letting your sinful nature control your mind leads to death. But letting the Spirit control your mind leads to life and peace.*

In order to have self-control, you must let God take control of your mind to help you fight against the desires you know are wrong.

Promise from God JAMES 1:12 | *God blesses those who patiently endure testing and temptation. Afterward they will receive the crown of life that God has promised to those who love him.*

SEX

What does God think about sex?

GENESIS 1:27-28 | *God created human beings in his own image . . . male and female he created them. Then God blessed them and said, "Be fruitful and multiply."*

GENESIS 2:24 | *A man leaves his father and mother and is joined to his wife, and the two are united into one.*

God created sex. He made man and woman sexual beings, with the ability to express love to and delight in each other and to reproduce and replenish the next generations. The sexual relationship is a key part of a husband and wife becoming one person. God intended sex to be a good thing within the context of the marriage relationship.

PROVERBS 5:18-19 | *Let your wife be a fountain of blessing for you. Rejoice in the wife of your youth. . . . Let her breasts satisfy you always. May you always be captivated by her love.*

SONG OF SONGS 7:6 | *Oh, how beautiful you are! How pleasing, my love, how full of delights!*

God clearly allows delight in sex within marriage. Sex is not for reproduction only, but also for a bonding of love and enjoyment between husband and wife.

Is it so bad if I just think about having sex with someone? I don't really do anything.

MARK 7:20-22 | *It is what comes from inside that defiles you. For from within, out of a person's heart, come evil thoughts, sexual immorality . . . lustful desires.*

What you think about doesn't come just from your mind; it comes from your heart as well. Your thoughts tell you the condition of your heart, and your every action begins as a thought. Left unchecked, wrong thoughts will eventually result in wrong actions. If you continue to think about having sex with someone, your heart will begin to convince your mind that what you want to do is okay. Sex was designed by God to be an integral part of the marriage relationship—and to be right in that context only.

But isn't my body my own, to do with as I choose?

1 CORINTHIANS 6:13 | *You can't say that our bodies were made for sexual immorality. They were made for the Lord, and the Lord cares about our bodies.*

1 CORINTHIANS 6:19-20 | *Don't you realize that your body is the temple of the Holy Spirit, who lives in you and was given to you by God? You do not belong to yourself, for God bought you with a high price. So you must honor God with your body.*

When you become a Christian, you dedicate yourself to the Lord, and that includes your body. It is no longer truly yours; it is his temple.

Why is virginity so important?

2 TIMOTHY 2:21 | *If you keep yourself pure, you will be a special utensil for honorable use. Your life will be clean, and you will be ready for the Master to use you for every good work.*

1 JOHN 3:3 | *All who have this eager expectation will keep themselves pure, just as he is pure.*

God gave you the gift of your virginity, and he allows you to choose to whom you will give it. You can give it to only one person in the whole world. Don't give this precious gift away to just anyone, but save it for the person who commits to you by marrying you. This is why God commands you to refrain from having sex before marriage—he is trying to protect you from people who will hurt you by stealing your purity without committing to you.

Promise from God 1 CORINTHIANS 10:13 | *The temptations in your life are no different from what others experience. And God* *is faithful. He will not allow the temptation to be more than you can stand. When you are tempted, he will show you a way out so that you can endure.*

SIN

What is sin?

ROMANS 3:23 | *Everyone has sinned; we all fall short of God's glorious standard.*

Sin is falling short of the standard of purity set forth by a holy God.

ROMANS 2:15 | *They demonstrate that God's law is written in their hearts, for their own conscience and thoughts either accuse them or tell them they are doing right.*

Sin is violating God's moral law.

ROMANS 6:12 | *Do not let sin control the way you live; do not give in to sinful desires.*

Sin is a power that seeks to influence, enslave, and destroy you.

ROMANS 7:21-23 | *I have discovered this principle of life—that when I want to do what is right, I inevitably do what is wrong. I love God's law with all my heart. But there is another power within me that is at war with my mind. This power makes me a slave to the sin that is still within me.*

Sin is warfare of the soul, a constant battle between good and evil inside you.

JAMES 4:17 | *It is sin to know what you ought to do and then not do it.*

Sin is not only doing wrong things but failing to do the right things.

What are the consequences of sin?

ISAIAH 59:2 | *It's your sins that have cut you off from God. Because of your sins, he has turned away and will not listen anymore.*

Sin alienates and separates you from God so that you are not able to enjoy a relationship with him.

ROMANS 6:23 | *The wages of sin is death.*

2 THESSALONIANS 1:9 | *[Those who don't know God and those who refuse to obey the Good News of our Lord Jesus] will be punished with eternal destruction, forever separated from the Lord and from his glorious power.*

Sin brings God's punishment because it is a violation of his laws and his holiness. Death is the penalty for your sins— spiritual death and eternal judgment by God.

Is everyone sinful?

PSALM 51:5 | *I was born a sinner—yes, from the moment my mother conceived me.*

ECCLESIASTES 7:20 | *Not a single person on earth is always good and never sins.*

ISAIAH 53:6 | *All of us, like sheep, have strayed away. We have left God's paths to follow our own.*

ROMANS 5:12 | *When Adam sinned, sin entered the world. Adam's sin brought death, so death spread to everyone, for everyone sinned.*

All people have sinned against God—everyone is born with a sinful nature. It is a condition present at birth and not something that can be avoided with the right training.

JEREMIAH 17:9 | *The human heart is the most deceitful of all things, and desperately wicked. Who really knows how bad it is?*

The human heart is far more sinful than you want to believe.

Is there a way to be free from sin?

PSALM 51:2-3 | *Wash me clean from my guilt. Purify me from my sin. For I recognize my rebellion; it haunts me day and night.*

PSALM 139:23-24 | *Search me, O God, and know my heart; test me and know my anxious thoughts. Point out anything in me that offends you, and lead me along the path of everlasting life.*

Ask God to cleanse your heart from sin.

ISAIAH 1:18 | *"Come now, let's settle this," says the LORD. "Though your sins are like scarlet, I will make them as white as snow. Though they are red like crimson, I will make them as white as wool."*

MATTHEW 26:28 | *[Jesus said,] "This is my blood, which confirms the covenant between God and his people. It is poured out as a sacrifice to forgive the sins of many."*

2 CORINTHIANS 5:21 | *God made Christ, who never sinned, to be the offering for our sin, so that we could be made right with God through Christ.*

COLOSSIANS 1:22 | *[God] has reconciled you to himself through the death of Christ. . . . As a result, he has brought you into* his own presence, and you are holy and blameless as you stand before him without a single fault.

God has made it possible for the stain of your sins to be removed because of the death and resurrection of Jesus Christ. He took the punishment you deserve for your sins so that your relationship with him can be restored. If you believe and accept what he did for you, he then looks at you as though you had never sinned.

1 JOHN 1:9 | *If we confess our sins to [God], he is faithful and just to forgive us our sins and to cleanse us.*

Confessing your sins to God and turning away from them to obey him is the only way to be free from sin's power and your guilt. When you confess your sins to God, he forgives you and forgets your sins.

ROMANS 6:6, 18 | *Our old sinful selves were crucified with Christ so that sin might lose its power in our lives. We are no longer slaves to sin. . . . You are free from your slavery to sin, and you have become slaves to righteous living.*

Because of Jesus' death and resurrection, once you accepted him as Savior you became free from the power of sin. This doesn't mean you will no longer sin, but that sin's power to enslave you has been defeated.

Am I really a Christian if I still sin?

JOHN 16:33 | *[Jesus said,] "I have told you all this so that you may have peace in me. Here on earth you will have many trials and sorrows. But take heart, because I have overcome the world."*

ROMANS 7:18-20 | *[Paul said,] "I know that nothing good lives in me, that is, in my sinful nature. I want to do what is right, but I can't. I want to do what is good, but I don't. I don't want to do what is wrong, but I do it anyway. But if I do what I don't want to do, I am not really the one doing wrong; it is sin living in me that does it."*

You will always struggle with sin, but if you place your faith in Jesus he guarantees victory over it.

1 JOHN 3:9 | *Those who have been born into God's family do not make a practice of sinning, because God's life is in them.*

Although as a believer you will still sin, by God's grace you are not dominated by the practice of sinning. True believers in Jesus no longer cling tenaciously to sin.

ROMANS 8:5 | *Those who are dominated by the sinful nature think about sinful things, but those who are controlled by the Holy Spirit think about things that please the Spirit.*

Sin loses its influence over you as you increasingly yield your life to the control of the Holy Spirit. The Spirit of God living in you reduces your appetite for sin and increases your hunger for God.

PSALM 119:11 | *I have hidden your word in my heart, that I might not sin against you.*

Knowing God's Word will enable you to refrain from sinning, for it contains the words from a holy God to guide you and protect you.

Promise from God 1 PETER 2:24 | *[Jesus] personally carried our sins in his body on the cross so that we can be dead to sin and live for what is right. By his wounds you are healed.*

SINGLENESS

Is God's plan for everyone to marry? Will I be missing out on his plan if I don't?

MATTHEW 19:12 | *Some choose not to marry for the sake of the Kingdom of Heaven.*

1 CORINTHIANS 7:7 | *Each person has a special gift from God, of one kind or another.*

Marriage or singleness can each be a gift from God. Is it all right to marry? Yes. Is it all right to remain single? Yes. There are advantages to both.

1 CORINTHIANS 7:32 | *An unmarried man can spend his time doing the Lord's work and thinking how to please him.*

In your singleness, serve the Lord wholeheartedly. Do not give in to the feeling that your life is incomplete without a spouse.

How can God help me accept my singleness?

1 CORINTHIANS 7:7-8 | *[Paul said,] "I wish everyone were single, just as I am. Yet each person has a special gift from God, of one kind or another. So I say to those who aren't married and to widows—it's better to stay unmarried, just as I am."*

1 CORINTHIANS 7:17 | *Each of you should continue to live in whatever situation the Lord has placed you.*

Sometimes, when you desperately want something, it is easy to forget the gifts of your current situation. Paul found that his singleness was an advantage in pursuing his call of establishing churches. Step back and think about how

God might want to use you while you are single or if you remain single.

How can I deal with loneliness?

1 CORINTHIANS 7:32 | *I want you to be free from the concerns of this life. An unmarried man can spend his time doing the Lord's work and thinking how to please him.*

You can alleviate loneliness by focusing your attention on what God wants you to be doing and by serving him whole-heartedly. Being alone doesn't have to equate to being lonely.

Promise from God EPHESIANS 2:19 | *You are members of God's family.*

SPIRITUAL WARFARE

What does the Bible say about spiritual warfare?

EPHESIANS 6:11-12 | *Put on all of God's armor so that you will be able to stand firm against all strategies of the devil. For we are not fighting against flesh-and-blood enemies, but against evil rulers and authorities of the unseen world, against mighty powers in this dark world, and against evil spirits in the heavenly places.*

Spiritual warfare is the unseen battle that is being waged for your soul and for your Christian testimony. Winning this battle requires preparation—through prayer, unwavering faith, and knowledge of biblical truth—to defeat your spiritual enemy.

1 PETER 5:8 | *Stay alert! Watch out for your great enemy, the devil. He prowls around like a roaring lion, looking for someone to devour.*

You must be alert at all times for the sneak attacks of the devil.

PHILIPPIANS 2:10 | *At the name of Jesus every knee should bow, in heaven and on earth and under the earth.*

JAMES 4:7 | *Resist the devil, and he will flee from you.*

When you resist the devil in the name and power of Jesus, he will flee from you. At the name of Jesus, Satan has no power.

MATTHEW 4:1, 3-4 | *Jesus was led by the Spirit into the wilderness to be tempted there by the devil. . . . During that time the devil came and said to him, "If you are the Son of God, tell these stones to become loaves of bread." But Jesus told him, "No! The Scriptures say . . ."*

When under attack by Satan, Jesus relied on the Word of God to combat the lies of his adversary.

Promise from God EPHESIANS 6:11 | *Put on all of God's armor so that you will be able to stand firm against all strategies of the devil.*

STRENGTHS/WEAKNESSES

How do I know my strengths and weaknesses?

1 CORINTHIANS 12:11 | *It is the one and only Spirit who distributes all these gifts. He alone decides which gift each person should have.*

EPHESIANS 1:16-17 | *I have not stopped thanking God for you. I pray for you constantly, asking God, the glorious Father of our Lord Jesus Christ, to give you spiritual wisdom and insight so that you might grow in your knowledge of God.*

Recognize that God is the source of your strengths and special abilities. He created you to serve him in a way unique from others by giving you special talents and abilities. Through prayer, God reveals your weaknesses and tells you how they can be strengthened.

1 TIMOTHY 4:14 | *Do not neglect the spiritual gift you received through the prophecy spoken over you when the elders of the church laid their hands on you.*

Often your strengths and weaknesses are more evident to others than to yourself. Seek the advice of others to help you determine what they are.

EXODUS 31:3 | *[The Lord said,] "I have filled him with the Spirit of God, giving him great wisdom, ability, and expertise in all kinds of crafts."*

ROMANS 12:6 | *In his grace, God has given us different gifts for doing certain things well. So if God has given you the ability . . . [do it] with as much faith as God has given you.*

Your strengths are probably those things that God has gifted you to do (see Romans 12:6-8).

Promise from God ISAIAH 40:29-31 | *[The Lord] gives power to the weak and strength to the powerless. Even youths will become weak and tired, and young men will fall in exhaustion. But those who trust in the LORD will find new strength. They will soar high on wings like eagles. They will run and not grow weary. They will walk and not faint.*

SUCCESS

What is true success in God's eyes?

MATTHEW 22:37 | *Jesus [said], "You must love the LORD your God with all your heart, all your soul, and all your mind."*

JOHN 15:8 | *[Jesus said,] "When you produce much fruit, you are my true disciples. This brings great glory to my Father."*

Success is loving God and living in a way that pleases him.

JOHN 17:3 | *This is the way to have eternal life—to know you, the only true God, and Jesus Christ, the one you sent to earth.*

ACTS 16:31 | *Believe in the Lord Jesus and you will be saved.*

Faith in Jesus is success because only through faith will you find salvation and eternal life.

JOSHUA 1:8-9 | *Study this Book of Instruction continually. Meditate on it day and night so you will be sure to obey everything written in it. Only then will you prosper and succeed in all you do. . . . For the LORD your God is with you wherever you go.*

PSALM 25:4-5 | *Show me the right path, O LORD; point out the road for me to follow. Lead me by your truth and teach me.*

Studying the Bible reveals God's will for your life, which is the most successful path you can take.

MATTHEW 20:25-26 | *Rulers in this world lord it over their people, and officials flaunt their authority over those under them. But among you it will be different. Whoever wants to be a leader among you must be your servant.*

Serving and helping others brings success in God's eyes.

JOHN 15:8, 16 | *When you produce much fruit, you are my true disciples. This brings great glory to my Father. . . . You didn't choose me. I chose you. I appointed you to go and produce lasting fruit, so that the Father will give you whatever you ask for, using my name.*

Success is being productive—producing results that matter to God.

PROVERBS 16:3 | *Commit your actions to the LORD, and your plans will succeed.*

Committing all you do to God brings success. Put God first in your life, for only then can you fully understand what is really important in life.

Promise from God PSALM 60:12 | *With God's help we will do mighty things.*

SUICIDE

Why is suicide wrong?

EXODUS 20:13 | *You must not murder.*

PSALM 119:73 | *You made me; you created me. Now give me the sense to follow your commands.*

God created you as a unique individual. It is he who breathed life into you and he alone who has the right to decide when your life should end. Taking your life is playing God—you are assuming that you know best when your life should end. Taking away God's gift of life demonstrates that you are no longer allowing him to be involved in your life.

Don't I have the final say over what happens to my body?

1 CORINTHIANS 3:16-17 | *Don't you realize that all of you together are the temple of God and that the Spirit of God lives in you? God will destroy anyone who destroys this temple. For God's temple is holy, and you are that temple.*

1 CORINTHIANS 6:12-13 | *You say, "I am allowed to do anything"— but not everything is good for you. And even though "I am allowed to do anything," I must not become a slave to anything. . . . [Our bodies] were made for the Lord, and the Lord cares about our bodies.*

Your life was given to you for the purpose of glorifying God. His Holy Spirit lives in your body. When you do things that are not good for your body or that destroy your body, you are breaking down the temple where God dwells.

Does God really have a plan for my life?

JEREMIAH 1:5 | *I knew you before I formed you in your mother's womb. Before you were born I set you apart and appointed you as my prophet to the nations.*

God has a perfect plan for your life, which he determined before you were even born. You must not play God by prematurely ending your life. If you were to take away your life, you would shortchange God's perfect plan because his work in and through you isn't finished yet.

Promise from God JEREMIAH 29:11 | *"I know the plans I have for you," says the LORD. "They are plans for good and not for disaster, to give you a future and a hope."*

TEMPTATION

Is temptation sin?

MATTHEW 4:1 | *Jesus was led by the Spirit into the wilderness to be tempted there by the devil.*

HEBREWS 4:14-15 | *Jesus . . . faced all of the same testings we do, yet he did not sin.*

Jesus was severely tempted, yet he never gave in to temptation. Since Jesus was tempted and remained sinless, we know that being tempted is not the same as sinning. You don't have to feel guilty about the temptations you wrestle with. Rather, you can devote yourself to resisting them.

Does my temptation ever come from God?

JAMES 1:13 | *When you are being tempted, do not say, "God is tempting me." God is never tempted to do wrong, and he never tempts anyone else.*

Temptation originates not in the mind of God but in the mind of Satan, who plants it in your heart. Victory over temptation originates in the mind of God and flows to your heart.

JAMES 1:2 | *When troubles come your way, consider it an opportunity for great joy.*

Although God does not send temptation, he brings good from it by helping you grow stronger through it.

Why is temptation so enticing to me?

GENESIS 3:6 | *The woman . . . saw that the tree was beautiful and its fruit looked delicious. . . . So she took some of the fruit and ate it.*

Satan's favorite strategy is to make that which is sinful appear to be desirable and good. In contrast, he also tries to make good look evil. If Satan can make evil look good and good look evil, then your giving in to temptation appears right instead of wrong. You must constantly be aware of the confusion he desires to create in you.

1 KINGS 11:1-3 | *Solomon loved many foreign women. . . . The LORD had clearly instructed the people of Israel, "You must not marry them, because they will turn your hearts to their gods." . . . And in fact, they did turn his heart away from the LORD.*

Often, temptation begins in seemingly harmless pleasure, soon gets out of control, and then progresses to full-blown sin. But the reality is that the kind of pleasure that leads to sin is never harmless. Before you give in to something that seems innocent, take a look at God's Word to see what it says. If Solomon had done this, he would have been reminded that his "pleasure" was really sin. Maybe he would have been convicted enough to stop.

How can I resist temptation?

1 TIMOTHY 4:7-8 | *Do not waste time. . . . Train yourself to be godly. "Physical training is good, but training for godliness is much better, promising benefits in this life and in the life to come."*

To overcome temptation, you need to prepare for it before it presses in on you. Train yourself in the quieter times so that you will have the spiritual wisdom, strength, and commitment to honor God in the face of intense desires and temptation.

GENESIS 39:12 | *She came and grabbed him by his cloak, demanding, "Come on, sleep with me!" Joseph tore himself away . . . [and] ran from the house.*

1 JOHN 5:21 | *Keep away from anything that might take God's place in your hearts.*

If possible, avoid or remove yourself from the tempting situation. Sometimes you must literally flee.

ECCLESIASTES 4:12 | *A person standing alone can be attacked and defeated, but two can stand back-to-back and conquer. Three are even better, for a triple-braided cord is not easily broken.*

Enlisting a Christian friend as an accountability partner will give you far more spiritual strength than you have on your own.

JAMES 4:7 | *Resist the devil, and he will flee from you.*

1 PETER 5:8-9 | *Stay alert! Watch out for your great enemy, the devil. He prowls around like a roaring lion, looking for someone to devour. Stand firm against him, and be strong in your faith.*

The devil has less power than you think. He can tempt you, but he cannot coerce you. He can dangle the bait in front of you, but he cannot force you to take it. You can resist the devil as Jesus did: by responding to the lies of the tempter with the truth of God's Word (see Matthew 4:1-11).

Promise from God 1 CORINTHIANS 10:13 | *The temptations in your life are no different from what others experience. And God is faithful. He will not allow the temptation to be more than you can stand. When you are tempted, he will show you a way out so that you can endure.*

TESTING

How is testing different from temptation?

1 PETER 1:7 | *These trials will show that your faith is genuine. It is being tested as fire tests and purifies gold—though your faith is far more precious than mere gold.*

Satan tempts you, trying to destroy your faith. God tests you to strengthen and purify it.

JAMES 1:3 | *When your faith is tested, your endurance has a chance to grow.*

Temptations try to make you give up. Testing tries to help you endure and not quit.

What good comes out of being tested?

GENESIS 22:1 | *God tested Abraham's faith.*

Out of testing comes a more committed faith. Just as commercial products are tested to strengthen their performance, so also God tests your faith to strengthen your resolve so you can accomplish all God wants you to.

JEREMIAH 6:27 | *[The Lord said,] "Jeremiah, I have made you a tester of metals, that you may determine the quality of my people."*

Spiritual testing reveals the impurities in your heart. Once you are able to recognize your sins and shortcomings, you can let God forgive and remove them, making you stronger and more pure.

DEUTERNOMY 13:3 | *The LORD your God is testing you to see if you truly love him with all your heart and soul.*

God's testing results in a deepening of your obedience and love for him.

DEUTERONOMY 8:2 | *Remember how the LORD your God led you through the wilderness for these forty years, humbling you and testing you to prove your character.*

Testing develops maturity of character. Character is strengthened not through ease but through adversity.

JAMES 1:2-4 | *When troubles come your way, consider it an opportunity for great joy. For you know that when your faith is tested, your endurance has a chance to grow. So let it grow, for when your endurance is fully developed, you will be perfect and complete, needing nothing.*

Testing develops endurance. It trains you to persist to the end rather than give up before you get there.

LUKE 8:13 | *The seeds on the rocky soil represent those who hear the message and receive it with joy. But since they don't have deep roots, they believe for a while, then they fall away when they face temptation.*

Testing reveals the strength of your commitment.

Promise from God JAMES 1:12 | *God blesses those who patiently endure testing and temptation. Afterward they will receive the crown of life that God has promised to those who love him.*

THANKFULNESS

Why should I give thanks to God?

1 CHRONICLES 16:34 | *Give thanks to the LORD, for he is good! His faithful love endures forever.*

Give thanks to God because he is always good and because he will always love you no matter what you've done. Thanking God for his character helps you more fully appreciate and respect the qualities in him and in others.

LUKE 17:16 | *He fell to the ground at Jesus' feet, thanking him for what he had done.*

A thankful heart grows your faith as you recognize God's work in your life.

1 CORINTHIANS 15:57 | *Thank God! He gives us victory over sin and death through our Lord Jesus Christ.*

Thank God because he gives you victory over sin and death when you put your faith in Jesus Christ.

COLOSSIANS 4:2 | *Devote yourselves to prayer with an alert mind and a thankful heart.*

Thank God because he answers prayer. Thankfulness in prayer acknowledges that God did something specific for you and that you are giving him the credit.

1 TIMOTHY 4:4 | *Since everything God created is good, we should not reject any of it but receive it with thanks.*

Thank God because the natural world he created is beautiful and good.

PSALM 111:1-2 | *Praise the LORD! I will thank the LORD with all my heart as I meet with his godly people. How amazing are the deeds of the LORD! All who delight in him should ponder them.*

By giving thanks to God, you can show others what he has done in your life and invited them into relationship with him.

HABAKKUK 3:17-19 | *Even though the fig trees have no blossoms, and there are no grapes on the vines; even though the olive crop fails, and the fields lie empty and barren; even though the flocks die in the fields, and the cattle barns are empty, yet I will rejoice in the LORD! I will be joyful in the God of my salvation! The Sovereign LORD is my strength!*

A spirit of gratitude and praise changes the way you look at life. Complaining connects you to your unhappiness—thankfulness and praise connect you to the source of real joy. When you make thanksgiving a regular part of your life, you stay focused on all God has done and continues to do for you. Expressing gratitude for God's help is a form of worship.

Promise from God 1 CHRONICLES 16:34 | *Give thanks to the LORD, for he is good! His faithful love endures forever.*

TOLERANCE

What things should I never tolerate?

DEUTERONOMY 7:2, 4-5 | *When the LORD your God hands these nations over to you and you conquer them, you must completely destroy them. Make no treaties with them and show them no mercy . . . for they will lead your children away from me to worship other gods. Then the anger of the* LORD *will burn against you, and he will quickly destroy you. This is what you must do. You must break down their pagan altars and shatter their sacred pillars. Cut down their Asherah poles and burn their idols.*

You must never tolerate idolatry and sin in your life. Society has many idols—not statues but other "gods" that take the priority the one true God should have in your life. Never allow devotion to idols into your heart.

2 CHRONICLES 18:1-2 | *Jehoshaphat enjoyed great riches and high esteem, and he made an alliance with Ahab of Israel by having his son marry Ahab's daughter. A few years later he went to Samaria to visit Ahab, who prepared a great banquet for him and his officials. They butchered great numbers of sheep, goats, and cattle for the feast. Then Ahab enticed Jehoshaphat to join forces with him to recover Ramoth-gilead.*

You should not be tolerant of evil or make alliances with those who are bent on doing evil. Never allow an attitude of tolerance to lead you into a position of moral or spiritual compromise.

EZRA 9:1 | *The Jewish leaders came to me and said, "Many of the people of Israel, and even some of the priests and Levites, have not kept themselves separate from the other peoples living in the land. They have taken up the detestable practices of the Canaanites, Hittites, Perizzites, Jebusites, Ammonites, Moabites, Egyptians, and Amorites."*

You should not be tolerant of adopting sinful lifestyle choices just because "everyone is doing it."

PSALM 101:5 | *I will not tolerate people who slander their neighbors. I will not endure conceit and pride.*

You should not tolerate pride in yourself. Pride clouds your judgment and your ability to distinguish right from wrong and truth from lies.

Promise from God DEUTERONOMY 8:19 | *If you ever forget the LORD your God and follow other gods, worshiping and bowing down to them, you will certainly be destroyed.*

TROUBLE

Is God listening when I cry out because of my troubles? Does he really hear, and does he care?

PSALM 18:6 | *In my distress I cried out to the LORD; yes, I prayed to my God for help. He heard me from his sanctuary; my cry to him reached his ears.*

MATTHEW 11:28 | *Jesus said, "Come to me, all of you who are weary and carry heavy burdens, and I will give you rest."*

God's hotline is always open. There is never a busy signal, and he is never too preoccupied with anything—even managing the universe—to listen to your every prayer and care about your every need. God has both a listening ear and a caring heart.

Will being faithful to God spare me from adversity?

DANIEL 3:16-20 | *Shadrach, Meshach, and Abednego replied, "O Nebuchadnezzar, we do not need to defend ourselves before you. If we are thrown into the blazing furnace, the God whom we serve is able to save us. . . . But even if he doesn't, we want to make it clear . . . that we will never serve your gods or worship the gold statue you have set up." Nebuchadnezzar was so furious . . . he commanded that the furnace be heated seven times hotter than usual. Then he ordered some of the strongest men of his army to bind Shadrach, Meshach, and Abednego and throw them into the blazing furnace.*

ACTS 5:17-18 | *The high priest and his officials . . . were filled with jealousy. They arrested the apostles and put them in the public jail.*

The lives of believers in both the Old and New Testaments testify that being faithful to God does not eliminate adversity. When you believe in Jesus, Satan becomes your enemy. He will try to stop you from following God by sending you all kinds of adversity. Recognize that it may be a sign that you are being faithful to God.

NAHUM 1:7 | *The LORD is good, a strong refuge when trouble comes. He is close to those who trust in him.*

In most cases, the Bible doesn't say *if* trouble will come, but *when* trouble comes. No one has lived his or her life without some adversity.

PSALM 27:5, 7-8 | *He will conceal me . . . when troubles come; he will hide me in his sanctuary. He will place me out of reach on a high rock. . . . Hear me as I pray, O LORD. Be merciful and answer me! My heart has heard you say, "Come and talk with me." And my heart responds, LORD, I am coming."*

Sometimes God does rescue you from adversity because of your faithfulness.

Is there any way I can avoid trouble and adversity?

JAMES 1:2-3 | *When troubles come your way, consider it an opportunity for great joy. For you know that when your faith is tested, your endurance has a chance to grow.*

Avoiding adversity may not be best for you. Though it may bruise you, it also can build you up and strengthen your faith.

PROVERBS 14:16 | *The wise are cautious and avoid danger; fools plunge ahead with reckless confidence.*

ROMANS 13:14 | *Clothe yourself with the presence of the Lord Jesus Christ. And don't let yourself think about ways to indulge your evil desires.*

The consequences of sin often bring unneeded adversity into your life. By obeying God's Word, you can avoid many kinds of adversity you might otherwise inflict on yourself.

PROVERBS 21:23 | *Watch your tongue and keep your mouth shut, and you will stay out of trouble.*

Controlling your tongue—using words wisely rather than unwisely—can help you avoid adversity.

PROVERBS 11:14 | *There is safety in having many advisers.*

Following advice from godly people will help you avoid trouble.

Promise from God PSALM 46:1 | *God is our refuge and strength, always ready to help in times of trouble.*

TRUTH

How does truth affect my relationship with God?

TITUS 1:2 | *[The truth] gives [those whom God has chosen] confidence that they have eternal life, which God—who does not lie—promised them before the world began.*

You can trust God because he always tells the truth. Nothing he has said in his Word, the Bible, has ever been proven wrong or false. He specifically created you in order to have a relationship with you for all eternity. If God says he loves you—and he always tells the truth—you can be sure he desires a relationship with you.

ISAIAH 33:15-16 | *Those who are honest and fair, who refuse to profit by fraud, who stay far away from bribes, . . . who shut their eyes to all enticement to do wrong—these are the ones who will dwell on high.*

Striving for honesty will help you experience the benefits of God's ultimate justice and protection.

Does God really expect me to tell the truth all the time?

EXODUS 20:16 | *You must not testify falsely against your neighbor.*

PROVERBS 6:16-17 | *There are six things the LORD hates—no, seven things he detests . . . a lying tongue . . .*

God's law clearly forbids intentional lying.

EPHESIANS 4:15 | *We will speak the truth in love.*

Followers of Jesus are called to speak the truth, always in a loving manner.

Why is telling the truth so important?

LUKE 16:10 | *If you are faithful in little things, you will be faithful in large ones. But if you are dishonest in little things, you won't be honest with greater responsibilities.*

Telling the truth is a litmus test to see if you are trying to model your life after the God of truth. If you are truthful in even small matters, you will have the reputation of being an honest person.

EPHESIANS 4:25 | *Stop telling lies. Let us tell our neighbors the truth, for we are all parts of the same body.*

Telling the truth promotes good relationships.

MATTHEW 12:33 | *A tree is identified by its fruit. If a tree is good, its fruit will be good. If a tree is bad, its fruit will be bad.*

Honest dealings reveal an honest character. What you do reveals who you are.

1 TIMOTHY 1:19 | *Cling to your faith in Christ, and keep your conscience clear. For some people have deliberately violated their consciences; as a result, their faith has been shipwrecked.*

Always telling the truth keeps a clear conscience.

PROVERBS 11:3 | *Honesty guides good people; dishonesty destroys treacherous people.*

There is freedom in honesty because you never have to worry about getting tripped up. Dishonesty and deception are a form of bondage because you get trapped by your lies.

Promise from God PSALM 119:160 | *The very essence of your words is truth; all your just regulations will stand forever.*

VALUES

Why should I take inventory of my values?

PROVERBS 30:8 | *Help me never to tell a lie.*

ROMANS 1:29 | *Their lives became full of every kind of wickedness, sin, greed, hate, envy, murder, quarreling, deception, malicious behavior, and gossip.*

EPHESIANS 5:4 | *Obscene stories, foolish talk, and coarse jokes—these are not for you. Instead, let there be thankfulness to God.*

How do you view actions (such as gossip, flattery, profanity, lying, or cheating) the Bible calls sin? If you don't see these as sin, you must face up to the fact that your values are different from God's.

MATTHEW 15:19 | *From the heart come evil thoughts, murder, adultery, all sexual immorality, theft, lying, and slander.*

The heart is the source of moral or immoral behavior. If your actions don't regularly match up with what God says is right, then you need a change of heart before you can change your behavior.

How do I cultivate godly values in myself?

MICAH 6:8 | *The LORD has told you what is good, and this is what he requires of you: to do what is right, to love mercy, and to walk humbly with your God.*

MATTHEW 7:12 | *Do to others whatever you would like them to do to you. This is the essence of all that is taught in the law and the prophets.*

GALATIANS 5:22-23 | *The Holy Spirit produces this kind of fruit in our lives: love, joy, peace, patience, kindness, goodness, faithfulness, gentleness, and self-control.*

Godly living simply means valuing what God values. If you want to have godly values, you need God living in you. He promises his Holy Spirit will literally live in you if you ask, helping you value what is truly important and then living it.

What are the benefits of living by the values God considers important?

1 SAMUEL 12:1, 3-4 | *Samuel addressed all Israel: . . . "Have I ever cheated any of you? Have I ever oppressed you? Have I ever taken a bribe and perverted justice?" "No," they replied, "you have never cheated or oppressed us, and you have never taken even a single bribe."*

2 KINGS 12:15 | *No accounting of this money was required from the construction supervisors, because they were honest and trustworthy men.*

Living by the values of Scripture earns you a good reputation, makes you trustworthy, and models the kind of life that pleases God.

Promise from God MICAH 6:8 | *O people, the LORD has told you what is good, and this is what he requires of you: to do what is right, to love mercy, and to walk humbly with your God.*

WEARINESS

What do I have to watch out for when I'm tired?

GALATIANS 6:9 | *Let's not get tired of doing what is good. At just the right time we will reap a harvest of blessing if we don't give up.*

Being tired makes you more susceptible to discouragement, temptation, and sin, and it causes you to lose hope that things will change in the future.

PROVERBS 30:1-2 | *I am weary, O God; I am weary and worn out, O God. I am too stupid to be human, and I lack common sense.*

Being tired causes you to lose perspective. When you're weary is not a good time to try to make important decisions.

JOB 10:1 | *I am disgusted with my life. Let me complain freely. My bitter soul must complain.*

Being tired can cause you to say things you may later regret.

ECCLESIASTES 1:8 | *Everything is wearisome beyond description. No matter how much we see, we are never satisfied. No matter how much we hear, we are not content.*

Being tired can cause you to lose your vision and purpose.

2 SAMUEL 17:1-2 | *Ahithophel urged Absalom, "Let me choose 12,000 men to start out after David tonight. I will catch up with him while he is weary and discouraged. He and his troops will panic, and everyone will run away. Then I will kill only the king."*

Weariness makes you vulnerable to your enemies. When your guard is down, it's easier for them to attack you.

Who can help me when I grow tired?

HABAKKUK 3:19 | *The Sovereign LORD is my strength! He makes me as surefooted as a deer, able to tread upon the heights.*

EPHESIANS 6:10 | *Be strong in the Lord and in his mighty power.*

When you are weary, tap into the Lord's power—it is not some fable or fairy tale, but real supernatural power from the One who created you and sustains you.

1 KINGS 19:5-8 | *As he was sleeping, an angel touched [Elijah] and told him, "Get up and eat!". . . So he ate and drank and lay down again. Then the angel of the LORD came again and touched him and said, "Get up and eat some more, or the journey ahead will be too much for you." So he got up and ate and drank, and the food gave him enough strength to travel.*

You can help yourself by taking good care of your body: exercise, rest, and eat nutritious meals. Poor nutrition and bad health habits invite burnout.

Promise from God MATTHEW 11:28 | *Jesus said, "Come to me, all of you who are weary and carry heavy burdens, and I will give you rest."*

WILL OF GOD

Does God have a plan for my life?

PSALM 139:3 | *You see me when I travel and when I rest at home. You know everything I do.*

God has both a general plan and a specific plan for your life. He wants you to follow a certain path toward his desired pur-pose for you, but he also cares about the details along the way.

PSALM 32:8 | *The LORD says, "I will guide you along the best pathway for your life. I will advise you and watch over you."*

God wants to help you follow the path that will be most pleasing to him, and in the long run, it will be the most fulfilling to you, too.

What are some things I can do to discover God's will for my life?

PROVERBS 2:3-5 | *Cry out for insight, and ask for understanding. Search for them as you would for silver; seek them like hidden treasures. Then you will understand what it means to fear the LORD, and you will gain knowledge of God.*

Give yourself completely to knowing his will. Seek God's will actively and passionately, not casually.

ISAIAH 2:3 | *Come, let us go up to the mountain of the LORD, to the house of Jacob's God. There he will teach us his ways, and we will walk in his paths.*

Let God teach you from his Word.

JAMES 1:5 | *If you need wisdom, ask our generous God, and he will give it to you. He will not rebuke you for asking.*

Pray, asking God to reveal his will to you.

ACTS 21:14 | *When it was clear that we couldn't persuade him, we gave up and said, "The Lord's will be done."*

Sometimes God's will for you becomes evident through circumstances beyond your control. You actively seek, but you allow God to work out his will in the way he deems best.

What are some of the things I can know are God's will for me?

AMOS 5:24 | *[The Lord said,] "I want to see a mighty flood of justice, an endless river of righteous living."*

God's will is that you seek justice at all times and do what is right.

1 CORINTHIANS 14:1 | *Let love be your highest goal!*

God's will is that you always love others.

MARK 10:45 | *Even the Son of Man came not to be served but to serve others and to give his life as a ransom for many.*

God's will is that you serve others, putting them above yourself.

GALATIANS 5:22-23, 25 | *The Holy Spirit produces this kind of fruit in our lives: love, joy, peace, patience, kindness, goodness, faithfulness, gentleness, and self-control. . . . Since we are living by the Spirit, let us follow the Spirit's leading in every part of our lives.*

God's will is that you live under the power and guidance of the Holy Spirit.

Promise from God JEREMIAH 29:11 | *"I know the plans I have for you," says the LORD. "They are plans for good and not for disaster, to give you a future and a hope."*

WISDOM

How will having wisdom help me?

ROMANS 12:2 | *Don't copy the behavior and customs of this world, but let God transform you into a new person by changing the way you think. Then you will learn to know God's will for you, which is good and pleasing and perfect.*

2 CORINTHIANS 10:4-5 | *We use God's mighty weapons, not worldly weapons, to knock down the strongholds of human reasoning and to destroy false arguments. We destroy every proud obstacle that keeps people from knowing God. We capture their rebellious thoughts and teach them to obey Christ.*

Wisdom transforms knowledge into commonsense action. Wisdom from God helps you develop a biblical outlook that penetrates the deceptive and distorted thoughts of the world.

PROVERBS 9:10 | *Fear of the LORD is the foundation of wisdom. Knowledge of the Holy One results in good judgment.*

Wisdom is not simply knowing facts and figures; it is also understanding the filter through which those facts and figures should be used. Wisdom recognizes that an all-powerful, all-knowing God has designed a moral universe with consequences for good or for sinful choices. Wisdom begins with understanding your accountability to and your full dependence on your Creator. It's not *what* you know, but *whom* you know.

How do I obtain wisdom?

JOB 28:12, 21 | *Do people know where to find wisdom? Where can they find understanding? . . . It is hidden from the eyes of all humanity.*

Wisdom is elusive unless you actively pursue it. When you know God, you know where to find it.

PSALM 5:8 | *Lead me in the right path, O LORD. . . . Make your way plain for me to follow.*

JAMES 1:5 | *If you need wisdom, ask our generous God, and he will give it to you. He will not rebuke you for asking.*

God promises to give wisdom to anyone who asks. You need not be embarrassed to ask God for the wisdom and direction you need.

PSALM 19:7 | *The instructions of the LORD are perfect, reviving the soul. The decrees of the LORD are trustworthy, making wise the simple.*

Obedience to God's Word—his commands, instructions, and teachings—will make you wise. The Bible is your most reliable source of wisdom and insight because it is the very counsel of God himself and therefore speaks to all situations.

1 CORINTHIANS 2:15-16 | *Those who are spiritual can evaluate all things, but they themselves cannot be evaluated by others. For, "Who can know the LORD's thoughts? Who knows enough to teach him?" But we understand these things, for we have the mind of Christ.*

Wisdom also comes from the Holy Spirit, who lives in you when you believe in Jesus Christ.

PROVERBS 20:18 | *Plans succeed through good counsel.*

Wisdom often comes to you through the counsel of thoughtful, godly people.

Promise from God PROVERBS 1:23 | *Come and listen to my counsel. I'll share my heart with you and make you wise.*

WITNESSING

How do I overcome my fear of witnessing? How will God help me be a witness to my faith?

MATTHEW 18:14 | *[Jesus said,] "It is not my heavenly Father's will that even one of these little ones should perish."*

Your commitment to witnessing begins by understanding that lost people matter to God.

EXODUS 4:12 | *[The Lord said,] "Now go! I will be with you as you speak, and I will instruct you in what to say."*

LUKE 21:15 | *[Jesus said,] "I will give you the right words and such wisdom that none of your opponents will be able to reply or refute you!"*

Trusting that God will speak through you will help you to overcome your fear of witnessing.

2 CORINTHIANS 4:11, 13 | *We live under constant danger of death because we serve Jesus, so that the life of Jesus will be evident in our dying bodies. . . . But we continue to preach because we have the same kind of faith the psalmist had when he said, "I believed in God, so I spoke."*

Even when you face death, faith in God can give you the courage to speak.

ACTS 18:9-10 | *One night the Lord spoke to Paul in a vision and told him, "Don't be afraid! Speak out! Don't be silent! For I am with you."*

You are not alone when you witness. God is there to give you the words and the strength to proclaim his message.

EZEKIEL 2:6 | *Do not fear them or their words. Don't be afraid even though their threats surround you like nettles and briers and stinging scorpions. Do not be dismayed by their dark scowls, even though they are rebels.*

Be strong in God, and realize that rejection is just part of the territory.

ACTS 4:18-20 | *They called the apostles back in and commanded them never again to speak or teach in the name of Jesus. But Peter and John replied, "Do you think God wants us to obey you rather than him? We cannot stop telling about everything we have seen and heard."*

Realize that when you witness you are following in Christ's and the apostles' footsteps.

ACTS 1:8 | *You will receive power when the Holy Spirit comes upon you. And you will be my witnesses, telling people about me everywhere—in Jerusalem, throughout Judea, in Samaria, and to the ends of the earth.*

The Holy Spirit will empower you and help you to speak.

1 CORINTHIANS 2:4 | *My message and my preaching were very plain. Rather than using clever and persuasive speeches, I relied only on the power of the Holy Spirit.*

Go ahead and speak, and the Holy Spirit will work in people's hearts and minds.

1 THESSALONIANS 2:4 | *Our purpose is to please God, not people. He alone examines the motives of our hearts.*

Focus on pleasing God rather than on pleasing people.

What do I do when people aren't interested in hearing about Christ?

ACTS 17:32-34 | *When they heard Paul speak about the resurrection of the dead, some laughed in contempt, but others said, "We want to hear more about this later." That ended Paul's discussion with them, but some joined him and became believers.*

The majority may seem disinterested or hostile, but you never know when someone will believe—so you should never give up.

EZEKIEL 2:5, 7 | *[The Lord said,] "Whether they listen or refuse to listen—for remember, they are rebels—at least they will know they have had a prophet among them. . . . . You must give them my messages whether they listen or not.*

Even if attitudes or circumstances are not favorable, courageously speak out anyway. In this way you honor God.

Promise from God LUKE 21:15 | *[Jesus said,] "I will give you the right words and such wisdom that none of your opponents will be able to reply or refute you!"*

WORK

How should I view work?

GENESIS 1:27-28 | *God created human beings in his own image. . . . Then God blessed them and said, "Be fruitful and multiply. Fill the earth and govern it. Reign over . . . all the animals."*

Know that there is value and honor in work. God created people and gave them dominion over his creation. In other words, God created you for work. Even before the Curse, humanity was given the opportunity to transform the raw materials of earth into things that would enhance life. Work has always been meant to honor the Lord, to give people the dignity of having something important to do, and to bring blessings to others.

1 THESSALONIANS 4:11-12 | *Make it your goal to live a quiet life, minding your own business and working with your hands, just as we instructed you before. Then people who are not Christians will respect the way you live, and you will not need to depend on others.*

Your attitude toward work should include the goal of honoring God by the way you work, as well as supporting yourself and others.

PROVERBS 13:11 | *Wealth from get-rich-quick schemes quickly disappears; wealth from hard work grows over time.*

Honest, hard work is much better than schemes to get rich quickly.

COLOSSIANS 3:17 | *Whatever you do or say, do it as a representative of the Lord Jesus, giving thanks through him to God the Father.*

Your goal is to work in such a way that you are a good representative of Jesus.

What if my work has nothing to do with anything "Christian"—how can God be glorified in my work?

GENESIS 2:2 | *On the seventh day God had finished his work of creation, so he rested from all his work.*

GENESIS 2:15 | *The LORD God placed the man in the Garden of Eden to tend and watch over it.*

Work is anchored in God's very character. Part of being made in God's image is sharing in the industrious and creative aspects of his nature—gardening was the very first job given to humans. Christians are needed in all kinds of vocations. Whatever your job, believe that God has placed you there for a reason, and then do your work well as a service to him and as a way to serve others.

COLOSSIANS 3:23 | *Work willingly at whatever you do, as though you were working for the Lord rather than for people.*

The way you approach work is evidence of your relationship to Christ.

Can I work too hard?

EXODUS 16:23 | *This is what the LORD commanded: Tomorrow will be a day of complete rest, a holy Sabbath day set apart for the LORD.*

MARK 6:31 | *Jesus said, "Let's go off by ourselves to a quiet place and rest awhile."*

There is a time to stop working in order to rest, to celebrate life, and to worship God.

Promise from God PHILIPPIANS 1:6 | *God, who began the good work within you, will continue his work until it is finally finished on the day when Christ Jesus returns.*

WORRY

How can I worry less?

PSALM 55:4-5 | *My heart pounds in my chest. . . . Fear and trembling overwhelm me, and I can't stop shaking.*

Worry and fear are normal responses to threatening situations, but often we imagine far worse scenarios than ever happen. Most of your worries never come true.

MATTHEW 6:27 | *Can all your worries add a single moment to your life?*

Instead of adding more time or better quality of life, worry diminishes your health and kills your joy.

PHILIPPIANS 4:6 | *Don't worry about anything; instead, pray about everything.*

1 PETER 5:7 | *Give all your worries and cares to God, for he cares about you.*

Talk to God openly about your worries. Hand them off to him as if to a consultant you totally trust or a supervisor in whom you have the utmost confidence.

PHILIPPIANS 4:8-9 | *Fix your thoughts on what is true, and honorable, and right, and pure, and lovely, and admirable. Think about things that are excellent and worthy of praise. . . . Then the God of peace will be with you.*

Fix your thoughts on the power of God, not the problems of life. Worry will always change you for the worse; God has the power to change you and your circumstances for the better. Turn your attention away from negative, unbelieving thoughts to positive, trusting thoughts.

EXODUS 14:13 | *Don't be afraid. Just stand still and watch the LORD rescue you today.*

Combat worry and anxiety by remembering and trusting what God, in his Word, has already promised to do for you.

Promise from God 1 PETER 5:7 | *Give all your worries and cares to God, for he cares about you.*

WORSHIP

Why is worship important to my relationship with God?

MICAH 4:2 | *Come, let us go up to the mountain of the LORD, to the house of Jacob's God. There he will teach us his ways, and we will walk in his paths.*

Something very powerful and unique happens when God's people get together to sing, praise, hear his Word, and worship him. There is a sense of community and fellowship that can happen only when believers worship together.

REVELATION 5:11-12 | *I heard the voices of thousands and millions of angels around the throne and of the living beings and the elders. And they sang in a mighty chorus: "Worthy is the Lamb who was slaughtered—to receive power and riches and wisdom and strength and honor and glory and blessing."*

Your worship of God is a foretaste of heaven.

How should I worship God?

PSALM 9:11 | *Sing praises to the LORD who reigns in Jerusalem. Tell the world about his unforgettable deeds.*

PSALM 35:18 | *I will thank you in front of the great assembly. I will praise you before all the people.*

Your worship should include giving praise and thanks to God for what he has done.

PSALM 147:1 | *Praise the LORD! How good to sing praises to our God! How delightful and how fitting!*

EPHESIANS 5:18-19 | *Be filled with the Holy Spirit, singing psalms and hymns and spiritual songs among yourselves, and making music to the Lord in your hearts.*

Music and singing are important parts of your worship to God.

HEBREWS 12:28 | *Since we are receiving a Kingdom that is unshakable, let us be thankful and please God by worshiping him with holy fear and awe.*

Holy fear and awe should be part of your attitude when worshiping.

MATTHEW 2:11 | *They entered the house and saw the child with his mother, Mary, and they bowed down and worshiped him. Then they opened their treasure chests and gave him gifts of gold, frankincense, and myrrh.*

Worship should be accompanied by giving.

How can I make worship a part of my daily life?

JOHN 4:24 | *God is Spirit, so those who worship him must worship in spirit and in truth.*

Worship is not confined to formal places and times. All that is required is that you worship God in spirit (through authentic faith inspired by the Holy Spirit) and in truth (according to God's true person and nature). You can do that anytime and anywhere.

Promise from God REVELATION 15:4 | *Who will not fear you, Lord, and glorify your name? For you alone are holy. All nations will come and worship before you, for your righteous deeds have been revealed.*

WORTH

Am I really important to God?

EPHESIANS 2:10 | *We are God's masterpiece. He has created us anew in Christ Jesus, so we can do the good things he planned for us long ago.*

PSALM 139:13 | *You made all the delicate, inner parts of my body and knit me together in my mother's womb.*

JEREMIAH 1:5 | *I knew you before I formed you in your mother's womb. Before you were born I set you apart and appointed you as my prophet to the nations.*

God made you with great skill and crafted you with loving care. He showed how much value he places on you by the way he made you.

PSALM 139:1-3 | *O LORD, you have examined my heart and know everything about me. You know when I sit down or stand up. You know my thoughts even when I'm far away. You see me when I travel and when I rest at home. You know everything I do.*

God values you so much that he watches over you no matter where you are or what you are doing. This tells you how special he thinks you are.

Promise from God GALATIANS 4:7 | *You are no longer a slave but God's own child. And since you are his child, God has made you his heir.*